al Kindi Abd al Masih ibn Ishak

The Apology of Al Kindy

Written at the Court of Al Mâmûn

al Kindi Abd al Masih ibn Ishak

The Apology of Al Kindy
Written at the Court of Al Mâmûn

ISBN/EAN: 9783744735124

Printed in Europe, USA, Canada, Australia, Japan

Cover: Foto ©ninafisch / pixelio.de

More available books at **www.hansebooks.com**

THE

APOLOGY OF AL KINDY.

WRITTEN AT THE COURT OF AL MÂMÛN,

(A.H. 215; A.D. 830)

IN DEFENCE OF
CHRISTIANITY AGAINST ISLAM.

With an Essay on its Age and Authorship read before the
Royal Asiatic Society.

BY

SIR WILLIAM MUIR, K.C.S.I., LL.D.,

AUTHOR OF "THE LIFE OF MAHOMET."

LONDON:
SMITH, ELDER & Co., 15 WATERLOO PLACE.
1882.

HERTFORD:

PRINTED BY STEPHEN AUSTIN AND SONS.

PREFACE.

I MAY say at once that my primary object, in the present undertaking, is to place the APOLOGY of AL KINDY in the hands of those who will use it in the interests of the Christian faith.

At the same time, apart from the religious aspect, the Apology possesses a very peculiar interest of its own. My attention was first directed to it by the Turkish Mission Aid Society, which printed very carefully the text from two imperfect manuscripts. A cursory perusal convinced me of its high dialectic merit, and also of its presumable authenticity, as belonging to the age—the third century of the Hegira (about 830 A.D.)—in which it purports to have been written. I accordingly published a short sketch, with a few extracts, in the INDIAN FEMALE EVANGELIST.[1]

Further study deepened the conviction. The Apology is quoted by the well-known writer Al Bîrûni (about 390 A.H.), as the Epistle of "Abd al

[1] *Indian Female Evangelist*, London, Nisbet and Co., April, 1881, Art. I.

Masîh *ibn Ishâc*, Al Kindy." This quotation, while proving the currency of the work in the century following that in which it was written, has given rise to a confusion, in the minds of some, between our Author and the famous Al Kindy (Abu Yûsuf Ibn Ishâc), "the Philosopher of Islam," who also flourished at the Court of Al Mâmûn. I was led therefore to inquire carefully into the question of authorship.

The "Philosopher" was unquestionably a professed Mahometan, which at once dispels the notion that he could have had any hand in the Apology. But the Beni Kinda (whence the title *Al Kindy*) formed a great clan of themselves, who, advancing from the south, spread over the centre and north of Arabia, and had, in the fifth and sixth centuries of the Christian era, a distinguished rôle in the history of the Peninsula.[1] At the rise of Islam, though the greater part of the tribe, headed by the celebrated Al Asháth, passed over to the faith of Mahomet, still a respectable minority appear to have continued their attachment to the Christian religion; and in the time of Al Mâmûn, this remnant must have afforded ample numbers to produce other men of distinction bearing the tribal title of *Kindy*, besides the great Philosopher. That our Author belonged to such a branch of the Kindy race, there is no reasonable doubt. And the internal evidence (apart altogether from that supplied by the quotation from Al Bîrûni) affords the strongest pre-

[1] See *Life of Mahomet* (1st edition), vol. i. p. clxxiii et seq.

sumption that the work is what it professes to be,—namely, an Apology in defence of the Christian religion in its polemical aspect, as opposed to the dominant Faith, at the Court of the Caliph Al Mâmûn. The Preliminary Essay is designed to establish this.

Apart from its literary and historical interest, however, the Apology can well afford to stand, as a controversial work, upon its own intrinsic merits. Notwithstanding a good deal that is weak in reasoning, some things that are even questionable in fact, and abundance of censorious epithets against the Moslem, Jewish, and Magian faiths that might well have been materially softened, yet, taken as a whole, the argument is, from the Apologist's stand-point, conducted with wisdom and ability; while throughout it is characterized by a singular mastery of the Arabic language. The treatment of Islam is so trenchant that the circulation of the Apology could hardly be tolerated in any of the effete and bigoted Mahometan states of the present day. And, indeed, excepting the Motázelite Caliphs, and perhaps also the great Akbar, I suppose there has been no Mahometan government in any age which would not have considered it a duty to suppress a work so dangerous to Islam, by the severest pains and penalties.[1] But as regards our own territories, the case is different. And certainly the appearance of an Apology written and circulated at the Court

[1] I am told by Dr. Lansing that by the old law of Egypt any house in which the MS. might be found was liable to be razed to the ground with forty houses round.

of an Abbasside Caliph, could hardly be objected to in the dominions of the Defender of the Christian faith.

With the view, therefore, of facilitating the use and translation of the Apology, or of selections from it, I have compiled a very full analysis of its contents, with a copious translation of the more interesting portions. In doing this, I have indicated a few passages which, for reasons specified, should be omitted. Whether there should be any further curtailment must depend on local considerations.

As an ancient and indigenous product of Asiatic Christianity, the Apology possesses not only a deep interest for ourselves, but it has also a practical bearing on the same controversy still being prosecuted in the East. The Christian Advocate there has it often thrown in his teeth that he is introducing a Christ whose features and teaching have been moulded after a European type; and whose religion, consequently, though suited to the Western, is alien from the Asiatic, mind and habit. This, at any rate, cannot be said of our Apologist. An Arab of the Arabs, born and bred a thousand years ago in the plains of Chaldæa, Al Kindy presents himself and his faith in a purely Asiatic dress and language. The objectors will find that the Gospel changes not with time or clime; and that neither in form nor substance, nor in the reasoning by which it is supported, does the Christianity of Al Kindy materially differ (excepting perhaps in the more fervid temperament and livelier fancy of the Asiatic disputant) from that which is put forth by the Missionary of the present day.

I have not sought to transfuse the eloquence of Al Kindy into these pages, but have confined myself to the substance and tenour of the argument. The discourse throughout is much abridged, and even where a passage is marked as a translation, the gist of the same is for the most part given in brief, and without the cumulation of epithets, and exuberance of verbiage, in which our Author delights. Even if I had the ability for the task, the differing genius of our language would have interfered with any attempt of mine at imitation. To form an adequate conception of the rushing flood of Al Kindy's rhetoric, the original must be read. Into Oriental languages, however, such as Persian and Urdoo, there should be little difficulty in transfusing both the style and the spirit of our Author.

It is now six-and-thirty years since, at the request of Dr. Pfander, I wrote an account of his three excellent Treatises on the Mahometan Controversy, in the Calcutta Review.[1] The effect produced by these, both in India and Turkey, has been not inconsiderable. But it is no disparagement of them to say that Al Kindy's Apology may be expected to cause a sensation incomparably more profound. That the champion of Christianity was himself a

[1] *Calcutta Review*, vol. viii. Art. VI.

native of the East, of noble Arab birth, and yet a Christian by descent, a philosopher, and an honoured attendant at the Court of the Caliph Al Mâmûn, must add prodigiously to the weight already attaching, from its intrinsic merits, to our Author's argument. Between this and Pfander's works, there is just the difference between perusing an essay, and hearing the warm and impassioned eloquence of the advocate in his own defence; between reading the description of a battle, and witnessing with your own eyes the hotly-contested field of the battle itself.

Grateful acknowledgment is due to the *Turkish Mission Aid Society*, for their ready appreciation of the value of the Apology, and the care taken in presenting us, notwithstanding the imperfection of the manuscripts, with a text so intelligently and carefully edited.

W. M.

1 *December*, 1881.

TABLE OF CONTENTS.

THE APOLOGY OF AL KINDY.

AN ESSAY ON ITS AGE AND AUTHORSHIP.

[*Read before the Royal Asiatic Society.*]

AL BÎRÛNI, in his *Vestiges of Ancient Nations*, written A.D. 1000 (A.H. 390), while describing the customs of the Sabeans, cites the authority of *Ibn Ishâc al Kindy, the Christian*, in these words:

"Likewise Abd al Masîh ibn Ishâc al Kindy, the Christian, in his reply to the Epistle of Abdallah ibn Ismaîl al Hâshimy, relates of them (the Sabeans) that they are notorious for Human sacrifice, but that at present they are not able to practise openly the same."[1]

A work answering the above description has recently been published by the Turkish Mission Aid Society, in Arabic, under the following title: *The Epistle of Abdallah ibn Ismaîl al Hâshimy to Abd al Masîh ibn Ishâc al Kindy, inviting him to embrace Islam; and the Reply of Abd al Masîh, refuting the same, and inviting the Hâshimite to embrace the Christian Faith.*

The book, we learn from a Note at the end, was printed from two MSS. obtained, one in Egypt, the other in Constantinople. Neither has the name of the copyist, nor the year of transcription. They are both said in this note, to be full

[1] *Chronology of Ancient Nations*, p. 187, by Dr. Sachau, London, 1879.
وكذلك حكي عبد المسيح بن اسحاق الكندي النصاري عنهم (اي الصابئه) في جوابه عن كتاب عبد الله بن اسماعيل الهاشمي انهم يعرفون بذبح الناس ولكن ذلك لا يمكنهم اليوم جهرا.

of errors and discrepancies. But the book has been edited with care and intelligence, and as a whole may be regarded as a correct reproduction of the original. The editor certainly deserves great credit for the way in which the task is executed. I proceed to give a brief account of the work.

The letters, themselves anonymous, are preceded by a short preface:

"*In the Name of* GOD, *the* ONE, *the* ETERNAL.

"It is related that in the time of ABDALLAH AL MÂMÛN, there lived a man of Hâshimite descent, and of Abbasside lineage, nearly related to the CALIPH. The same was famed, among high and low, for devotion to Islam, and the careful observance of all its ordinances. This person had a friend, learned and virtuous, endowed with the gifts of culture and science, of pure and noble descent from the BENI KINDA, and distinguished for his attachment to the Christian faith. The same was in the service of the Caliph, and nigh unto him in honour and dignity. Now these two men had a mutual love, and an implicit trust in the friendship of each other. AL MÂMÛN, Commander of the Faithful, moreover, and his whole Court, were aware of it. But we are averse from mentioning their names, lest it should do harm. The HÂSHIMITE wrote to the Christian a letter, of which this is a copy."[1]

[1] I subjoin the Arabic text:

بسم اللّٰه الواحد الصمد

ذكر انه كان في زمن عبد اللّٰه المامون رجل من نبلآء الهاشميين واظنه من ولد العباس قريب القرابة من الخليفة معروفٌ بالنسك والورع والتمسك بدين الاسلام وشدة الاغراق فيه والقيام بفرائضه وسننه مشهورٌ بذلك عند الخاصة والعامة وكان له صديق من الفضلآء ذو ادب وعلم كنديٌّ الاصل مشهور بالتمسك بدين النصرانية وكان في خدمة الخليفة وقريبًا منه مكانا فكانا يتوادّان ويتحابّان ويثق كل منهما بصاحبه وبالاخلاص له وكان امير المؤمنين المامون وجماعة اصحابه والمتصلون به قد عرفوهما بذلك وكرهنا ان نذكر اسميهما لعلة من العلل فكتب الهاشمي الي النصراني كتابًا هذه نسخته.

The Hâshimite's letter follows immediately on this. He reminds his friend that he is himself well versed in the Scriptures, and in the practices and doctrines of the various Christian sects; and he proceeds to explain the teaching of Islam, and to press its acceptance on him. He begs of his friend to reply without fear or favour, and promises the guarantee of the Caliph that no harm should befall him for any freedom of speech in discussing the merits of their respective faiths. The reply of Al Kindy is introduced thus:

And the Christian answered him:

IN THE NAME OF GOD MOST MERCIFUL!

O Lord make my task easy: let it not be hard: and fulfil the same with thy blessing.

"To N—, son of N—, from M—, son of M—, the least of the servants of the Messiah. Peace, Mercy, and Grâce be upon thee, and upon all mankind! Amen."

And thereupon he proceeds to take up his friend's arguments, point by point.

The Moslem's letter occupies only twenty-two pages; Al Kindy's reply the remaining 142. While our Apologist speaks respectfully of the person of Mahomet, he vigorously denounces his claims as a prophet, and attacks the whole system of Islam with uncompromising severity. The latter part of the Apology is devoted to the proofs of Christianity, and our Saviour's life and teaching. The reasoning is not, to our ideas, uniformly sound; nor are the facts (throughout deeply tinged with Alyite and Abbasside tendencies), especially those connected with the life of the Prophet and the early Caliphate, always accurate. But upon the whole the argument is conceived with great ability and force, and the language throughout is flowing, rich, and eloquent. Many passages, in particular the philippic on Jehâd and Martyrdom, are singularly powerful and impassioned. It is clear that the Apology can have proceeded from the pen of no ordinary scholar.

There is no doubt that this book is substantially the same as that referred to by Al Bîrûni. At page 26 will be found the passage quoted by him as noticed at the beginning of this paper. Our Apologist there writes:

"We know from the Book of Genesis that Abraham lived with his people four-score years and ten, in the land of Harrân, worshipping none other than Al Ozza, an idol famous in that land, and adored by the men of Harrân under the name of the Moon, which same custom prevails among them to the present day. They conceal no part of their ancestral practices, save only the sacrifice of human beings. They cannot now offer up human sacrifices openly; but they practise the same in secret."[1]

In the brief Preface, it will have been observed that the correspondence is said to have taken place at the Court of Al Mâmûn (198–218 A.H.). At the close of the Egyptian MS. is the following Note:

"It is related that the subject of these two Epistles reached the ears of Al Mâmûn; whereupon he sent for them, and had them both read to him without stopping, from beginning to end. He then declared that he had no ground for interference, nor any cause against the Christian apologist. There are (added the Caliph) two religions—one for this world, the Magian, following the precepts of Zoroaster; the other for the world to come—the Christian, following the precepts of the Messiah. But the true religion is that of the Unity taught by our Master. That verily is the religion which serveth both for this life and the next."—p. 165.

This note is wanting in the Constantinople MS. It is no doubt an addition to the Treatise as originally put forth; but of what antiquity and authority there is no ground for saying.

It is otherwise with the short Preface, which is the same in both MSS., and probably formed the Introduction to the Discussion as it at first appeared. Excepting, however, that it gives the name of the Caliph, the preface adds nothing to what we gather from the Epistles themselves of the person-

[1] لا يكاتمون بها ولا يسترون منها شيئًا غير القرابين التي يتخذونها من الناس فان ذبح الناس لا يتهيّأ لهم اليوم جهرًا بل يحتالون فيه فيفعلون سرًّا.

ality of the disputants, namely, that both lived at the Court of the Caliph; that the Mahometan was the cousin of the Caliph, a Hâshimite of Abbasside lineage; and that the Christian was a learned man at the same Court, of distinguished descent from the tribe of the Beni Kinda, and held in honour and regard by Al Mâmûn and his nobles. But the names and further identification of the disputants are withheld, from motives of prudence,—"in case it might do harm."

From the passage in Al Bîrûni, however, it is evident that in his time (390 A.H.) the Discussion was currently received under the title, "The Reply of Abd al Masîh *Ibn Ishâc* al Kindy, to the Epistle of Abdallah *ibn Ismaîl* al Hâshimy." The epithets Abdallah and Abd al Masîh are of course *noms de plume*. It is possible that the other names (in italics) are so also;—Isaac and Ishmael symbolizing the Christian and Moslem antagonists.

Whether this be so or no, the name of *Ibn Ishâc al Kindy* has occasioned the surmise in some quarters that our Apologist was the same as the famous "Philosopher of Islam," Abu Yûsuf ibn Ishâc al Kindy, who also flourished at the Court of Mâmûn and his Successor. There can, however, be little or no doubt that the famous Al Kindy was a Mahometan by profession. As a *Failsûf*, or philosopher, he was, it may be, not a very orthodox professor; but, at any rate, there is no reason to suppose that he had any leaning towards Christianity: on the contrary (as we shall see below), he wrote a treatise to refute the doctrine of the Trinity. His father, or grandfather, was governor of Kûfa, a post that could be held by none other than a Mahometan; and Al Ashâth, the renowned chief of the Beni Kinda, who was converted in the time of Mahomet, and married Abu Bekr's sister, is said to have been his ancestor; whereas our Apologist glories in his Christian ancestry.

On the philosopher Al Kindy, de Sacy gives us an interesting note. After showing that D'Herbelot was mistaken in calling him a Jew,[1] and citing the authority of Abul Faraj and Ibn Abi Oseiba for regarding him as a Mussul-

[1] On this, see notes in Slane's Ibn Khallicân, vol. i. pp. xxvii and 355.

man, he mentions three considerations which might be urged against this view. *First:* In the catalogue of his writings there is none relating to the Coran or to Islam. *Second:* Al Kindy was one of the translators of Aristotle, familiar with Greek and Syriac; and men of that stamp were mostly Christians. *Third:* In the Bibliothèque Impériale there is a MS. (257) entitled A Defence of the Christian Religion (apparently identical with our Apology), written in Syriac characters, but in the Arabic language, the author of which is named *Yácûb Kindi.*

"Of these objections (continues de Sacy) the last alone merits attention; but it may be met by these counter-considerations. In the Preface the author is not named. The work is only said to have been written by a person attached to the court of Al Mâmûn, a Christian of Kindian descent. It is called 'The Treatise of Al Kendy, *the Jacobite.*'[1] It is most likely by a misunderstanding, or with the view of increasing thereby the value of the work, that it has been ascribed to the authorship of Yácûb Kindy. This suspicion acquires greater force, as in the catalogue of Syrian writers, written by Ebed Jesu, we find a certain Kendi named as the author of a religious treatise; and the Kendi in question (the same without doubt as the writer of our Syrian MS. (257), or at least whose name has been assumed as such) lived, according to an historian cited by Assemanus, about 890 A.D. (280 A.H.), a date to which it is little likely that Yacub Kendi survived. . . . For the rest we may suppose that Kendi, in pursuit of his philosophical studies, had embraced opinions opposed to Mahometan orthodoxy, and that this led to his faith being suspected—a thing which has occurred to many Christian philosophers, and among the Jews happened to the famous Maimonides."[2]

But this *Kendi* of Ebed Jesu, whoever he was, could not possibly have been our Apologist, for he flourished towards the end of the third century of the Hegira, whereas the Apology (as I hope to establish below) was certainly written during the reign of Al Mâmûn, near the beginning of that century. The passage from Assemanus, referred to by de

[1] كتاب الكندي اليعقوبي. This, of course, is a mistake, as our Apologist was a staunch Nestorian. There may have been some other Kendy a Jacobite; or rather the epithet *ibn Yácûb* has been so misunderstood and misapplied.

[2] Relation de L'Egypte par Abd Allatif, M. de Sacy, Paris, 1810, p. 487.

Sacy, consists of a note on chapter cxlii. of Ebed Jesu's Catalogue (in Syriac verse) of Christian authors. The verse and note are as follows:

[VERSE.]—"CANDIUS *fecit ingens volumen Disputationis et Fidei.*

[NOTE.]—"Candius, ابن كندا, Ebn Canda, hoc est Candiae filius; who flourished under the Nestorian Patriarch Joannes IV., A.D. 893. Others refer the authorship to Abu Yûsuf Yâcûb ibn Ishâc al Kindi; but he, according to Pocock and Abul Faraj, was a Mahometan . . . But the Candius whom Ebed Jesu mentions was a Nestorian, not a Mahometan, and wrote in the Syrian language, not in Arabic."[1]

If any doubts were entertained of the religious principles of Abu Yûsuf ibn Ishâc, they must be set at rest by the fact that he wrote a treatise to disprove the doctrine of the Trinity. It was answered by Yahya ibn Adî, a Jacobite writer, whose pamphlet appears as No. 108 in Steinschneider's list.[2] The same is in the Vatican Library (Codex, 127, f. 88), and was kindly copied out for me by Prof. Ign. Guidi. In this tract, the attack of Ibn Ishâc is quoted and replied to passage by passage; and the tenor of the writing leaves no doubt of the antagonism of the writer to Christianity.

On all these grounds, we must clearly look for the author of our Apology elsewhere.[3] But before doing so, it may be expedient to notice the conjecture of de Sacy, that the Apology may have been ascribed to Abu Yûsuf ibn Ishâc al Kindy, either by a misunderstanding, or as a pious fraud with the view of gaining for it greater celebrity and weight.

As to the supposed misunderstanding, it seems doubtful whether, in reality, the Apology ever was so ascribed, except-

[1] Bibliotheca Orientalis, Assemani, A.D. 1725, vol. iii. p. 213. The assumption that he wrote in Syriac is unfounded. But the treatise was probably translated into that language, as well as transliterated from the original into Syriac writing.

[2] Pol. und Apolog. Literatur in Arab. Sprache, Leipzig, 1877, p. 126.

[3] Those who care to prosecute the inquiry further, will find an elaborate article on *Al Kindi der Philosoph der Araber*, Ein Vorbild seiner Zeit und seiner Volkes, by Dr. G. Flügel, Leipzig, 1857. The paper is founded mainly on the authority of Ibn Abi Oseiba and Ibn Kufti, and is learned and exhaustive. A curious astrological treatise by the same Al Kindy is given by Dr. Otto Loth, p. 261, *Morgenländische Forschungen*, Leipzig, 1875. The cycles of Arabian history are there ascribed to astronomical conjunctions, and the essay closes with a prophecy of the eventual ascendancy of Islam over all other faiths.

There is also a short article with an exhaustive list of Ibn Ishâc's works, by Ibn Joljol, the Spanish writer, in the Bibliotheca Escurialensis, Casiri, Matriti, 1760 A.D. vol. i. p. 357.

ing as a mere conjecture in modern times. The misunderstanding, whatever it may have been, has arisen apparently from the similarity of name and tribe, as given in the quotation by Al Bîrûni.

The notion that, with the view of gaining greater weight, a paper purporting to be in refutation of Islam and establishment of Christianity, should have been ascribed to a Mahometan philosopher, will hardly, I think, be seriously held. What possible advantage could have been expected from an attempt to palm off a polemical work of the kind on an enemy of the Christian faith, who had himself attacked one of its cardinal doctrines? There is, moreover, no trace in the Apology itself of any design to rest upon the authority of a great name. The writer's identity, as we have seen, is carefully suppressed. The only thing common to the "Philosopher" and the Author, which appears throughout the work, is that the Author was learned, and went by the tribal title of *Al Kindy;* but that tribe was surely numerous and distinguished enough to embrace other men of letters and noble birth at the Court of Al Mâmûn. Leaving now the "Philosopher," we may proceed, therefore, to consider the internal evidence furnished by the book itself of its age and authorship.

I have said that the name of AL MÂMÛN, though given in the Preface, occurs nowhere in the Epistles themselves. But the manner in which the Caliph is throughout referred to, accords entirely with the assumption that they were written at his Court. He is spoken of as the paternal cousin of the Moslem writer; his just and tolerant sway is repeatedly acknowledged by Al Kindy; the descent of the Dynasty from the family of Mahomet is over and again referred to, and our Author prays that the Empire may long be perpetuated in his Patron's line. All this is perfectly natural, and in entire consistency with the ascription of the work to a courtier in the reign of Al Mâmûn.

Not less remarkable are the propriety and accuracy of all the historical notices. For example, when tracing the fate of the four Examplars of the Coran deposited by Othmân in the chief cities of the Empire, our Apologist tells us that the copy at Medîna disappeared in "the reign of terror, that is, in the days of Yezîd ibn Muâvia"; and that the manuscript at Mecca was lost or burnt in the sack of that city by Abu Sarâya, "the *last attack* made upon the Káaba."[1] This is exactly what a person writing some fifteen years after the event, and in the reign of Al Mâmûn, would say; for the siege of Mecca was then, in point of fact, the last which had taken place, under the insurgent Abu Sarâya, in the year 200 A.H. Had the Apology been written later on, say in the fourth century, the "latest attack" on Mecca would not have been that of Abu Sarâya, but of Soleimân Abu Tâhir in 317 A.H. So also, in illustrating the rapine and plunder of the early Moslem campaigns, Al Kindy mentions, as of a similar predatory and ravaging character, the insurrection of Bâbek Khurramy, and the danger and anxiety it occasioned thereby "to our lord and master the Commander of the Faithful." This rebellious leader, as we know, had raised the standard of revolt in Persia and Armenia some years before, routed an army of the Caliph, and long maintained himself in opposition to the Imperial forces; and the notice, as one of an impending danger then occupying men's minds, is precisely of a kind which would be natural and apposite at the assumed time, and at no other.[2] Once more, in challenging his friend to produce a single prophecy which had been fulfilled since the era of Mahomet, he specifies the time that had elapsed as "a little over 200 years," and uses the exact expression to denote the period, which would fall from the pen of a person writing about the era, 215 A.H., when we assume the work to have been written.[3] While the incidental references to dates and historical facts are thus in exact and happy keeping with the professed age of the

[1] p. 81.

[2] p. 47. The name is erroneously printed اتابك الخزمي. But there can be no doubt that Bâbek Khurramy بابك خرمي is the correct reading.

[3] لان هذه نيف ومائتا سنة قد مضت من ذلك الوقت. The words imply "two hundred and odd years," or a little over 200. The edict against the eternity of the Coran was issued I think about the year 211 or 212 A.H.; and our Discussion took place probably a year or two later, say 215 A.H.

work, there is throughout not a single anachronism or forced and unnatural allusion,—which in a person writing at a later period, and travelling over so large a field, would hardly have been possible.

Still more striking are the aptness and propriety of the political allusions. These are in the strictest affinity, not only with the traditions of an Abbasside Dynasty, but of a Court which had become partizan of the Alyite faction, which freely admitted Motázelite or latitudinarian sentiments, and which had just declared the Coran to be created and not eternal. The Omeyyad race are spoken of with virulent reprobation; the time of Yezîd is named the "reign of terror"; and Hajjâj, with his tyranny and the imputation of his having corrupted the Coran, is referred to in the bitter terms that were current in that day. Abu Bekr, Omar, and Othmân are treated as usurpers of the Divine right of succession which (it is implied) vested in Ali. I need hardly point out how naturally all this accords with the sentiments predominating at the Court of Al Mâmûn; but which certainly would not have been tolerated some forty or fifty years later.[1]

The freedom of our Author's treatment of Islam would have been permitted at none but the most latitudinarian Court. He casts aside the prophetical claims of Mahomet, censures some of his actions in the strongest language, reprobates the ordinances of Islam, especially those relating to women, and condemns Jehâd with scathing denunciation. It is difficult to conceive how such plain-speaking was tolerated even at the Court of Al Mâmûn; at any other, the Apology would have had small chance of seeing the light, or the writer of escaping with his head upon his shoulders. That the work did (as we know) gain currency can only have been due to its appearance at this particular era.

These remarks apply with very special force to the section on the Coran, since it seems highly probable that the Apology was written shortly after the famous edict of Al Mâmûn which denied the eternity of the Moslem Scriptures. The composition of the Coran is assailed by

[1] See my Rede Lecture on the *Early Caliphate*, Smith and Elder, 1881, p. 21.

our Author in the most incisive style. First, a Christian Monk inspired it, and then Rabbis interpolated it with Jewish tales and puerilities. It was collected in a loose and haphazard way. Besides the authorized edition imposed by the tyranny of Othmân (and subsequently depraved by Hajjâj),[1] Ali, Obey ibn Káb, and Ibn Masûd, had each their separate exemplars. Having been compiled, if not in part composed, by different hands, and thrown unsystematically together, the text is alleged to be in consequence full of contradictions, incoherencies, and senseless passages. A great deal of this section, though in less irreverential language, was no doubt very similar to the kind of arguments held by the rationalistic Motázelites of the day, and favoured by Al Mâmûn. For we know that it was after a hot and prolonged discussion that the Coran was proclaimed by Al Mâmûn to be created. It is therefore altogether in accord with the probabilities of the case, that this particular phase of the argument should have been (as we actually find it) treated by our Author at great length and with a profusion of tradition possessing little authority, although popular in that day,—a kind of rank mushroom growth springing out of Abbasside faction. The tables were soon turned on this free-thinking generation, who in their turn suffered severe persecution; and never before or afterwards did such an opportunity occur, as our Apologist enjoyed, under the very shadow of a Caliph's Court, to argue out his case with his enemy's weapons ready to his hand.

Al Kindy makes a strong point of the hypocrisy of the Jews and Bedouins who lived at the rise of Islam, their superficial conversion, and the sordid and worldly motives by which, when the great Apostacy followed the Prophet's death, they were brought back to Islam, "some by fear and the sword, some tempted by power and wealth, others drawn by the lusts and pleasures of this life." It was just the same,

[1] The action of Al Hajjâj (who has been sufficiently misrepresented and abused by the Abbasside faction) appears to have been mainly confined to certain additions in the way of diacritical marks. See Slane's Ibn Khallikân, vol. i. p. 359 and note 14, p. 364. But it was natural, at an Abbasside Court, to vilify that great, but stern, Viceroy of the Omeyyads.

he said, with the Jews and Magians of his own day. And to make good his point he proceeds to quote a speech of the Caliph, made in one of the assemblies which he was in the habit of holding. The passage is so remarkable, and so illustrative of the character of Al Mâmûn, that, at the risk of lengthening my paper, I give it here in full :—

SPEECH OF AL MÂMÛN.

And I doubt not but (the Lord bless thee, my Friend!) thou rememberest that which passed at an assembly of the Commander of the Faithful, to whom it had been related in respect of one of his Courtiers that, though outwardly a Moslem, he was at heart a reprobate Magian: whereupon the Caliph delivered himself (as I have been informed) in the following terms:

"By the Lord! I well know that one and another (and here the Caliph named a whole company of his Councillors), though professing Islam, are free from the same; they do it to be seen of me; while their convictions, I am well aware, are just the opposite of that which they profess. They belong to a class who embrace Islam, not from any love of this our religion, but thinking thereby to gain access to my Court and share in the honour, wealth, and power of the Realm; they have no inward persuasion of that which they outwardly profess. Truly their case, to my mind, resembleth the too common one of the Jews, who, when Islam was promulgated, held by the Tourât and the Law of Moses. And, indeed, I know of one and another (here the Caliph named a whole band of his Courtiers) who were Christians, and embraced Islam unwillingly. They are neither Moslems nor Christians, but impostors. And how shall I deal with these, seeing that the curse of God is upon them all? When they abandoned the Magian religion (the vilest and most abominable of all religions), it was incumbent on them to hold firmly by the new religion which they embraced, instead of by that which they left only in appearance and hypocrisy; and so likewise, with those who abandoned the Christian faith (the most amenable of all religions to the effulgence of Islam and the truth of its creed). But herein, I have the example and precedent of the Prophet (on whom be blessing![1]). For many of his companions, and familiars, and near of kin professed to follow him and be his Helpers; whilst he (on whom be blessing!) knew well

[1] This pious salutation at mention of the Prophet, universal among the Mahometans, occurs only here in the Caliph's address, and not in any other part of our Author's writing.

enough that they were all the time hypocrites, opposed at heart to what they outwardly professed. These ceased not to study evil, and to plot, to seek his fall, and to assist the Idolators against him; insomuch that a company of them lay in wait at a certain pass to affright his mule, so that it might throw him, and he be killed. But the Lord delivered and protected him from their snares, and the evil they thought to visit him with. Notwithstanding, he intreated them courteously to the end, even until the Lord took his spirit unto himself. Thus he guarded himself by kindness and courtesy against their machinations. Wherefore, it well becometh me that I should follow his example. Then after his death they all apostatized, seeking both outwardly and in their hearts, both in secret and in public, to scatter Islam and destroy the empire; until, at the last, the Lord helped the same, and healed the schisms; and that he did by casting into the hearts of certain amongst them the lust of empire and love of the world; and so the government was strengthened and the divisions reconciled, by means of kindness and forbearance. Thus the Lord fulfilled that which he hath fulfilled for us; and herein, no thanks or praise to any but to the Lord alone! Now, therefore, I will no more make mention of that which I have seen and heard in respect of these my Courtiers; but I shall treat them with courtesy and forbearance until the Lord decide between us, and *he is the best of all deciders.*"

Now, unless my lord, the Commander of the Faithful, had spoken thus openly in the ears of the nobles at his Council (the Lord exalt the same!), and the tidings thereof had spread, and the present ones had told the absent ones, I had not ventured to make mention of it here. Thou art witness that I have not added one thing thereto. And I only remind thee now (for no long time has elapsed) of that which passed at this assembly, in order to bring up clearly the subject of the great Apostacy, and to show that the people were not reconverted therefrom unto Islam, but through love of the world, and to build up this Empire under which they now live. In proof thereof, if the Lord will, this answer will suffice for all enlightened persons who may peruse my book.—Page 66.

It may appear strange that the Caliph should have expressed himself in this outspoken way regarding many of his Courtiers in a public assembly. But, certainly, the sentiments are in entire accord with what we know of the character and principles of Al Mâmûn, and also with the social and religious elements prevailing at Merve, where he first assumed the Caliphate, as well as at Baghdad, where he shortly after fixed his Court. It is difficult to believe that any one would have ventured to fabricate such a speech; or, supposing it genuine, that it should have been quoted by other than a contemporaneous writer.

I proceed to notice what evidence there is in the Epistles that the disputants were what they profess to have been, that is, persons of some distinction at the Court of AL MÂMÛN. The Apology, it is true, from its antiquity and rhetoric, may well stand upon its own intrinsic merit; but, undoubtedly, the controversy is invested with fresh life and interest when we know that the combatants were not fictitious, but real personages.

First, as regards *the Hâshimite;* it is conceivable, of course, that he is an imaginary person, set up to be aimed at as the representative of Islam; a mere catspaw, to draw forth the Christian's argument. This was the surmise of one of the learned Ulema from Constantinople, to whom I showed the book; but his chief reason for so thinking was that the argument for Islam was weakly stated, and that a much better case might have been made out.[1] In opposition to this view, it may be observed that the personality and character of the Moslem are sustained consistently throughout both Epistles. Every notice and allusion is in keeping with his assumed Hâshimite and Abbasside descent, his relationship to the Caliph, his friendship for our Apologist, and the guarantee of freedom and safety obtained by him for the discussion. There is besides more than one incident of personal life. Thus we have a curious passage on the use of the Cross, in which Al Kindy reminds his friend that repeatedly in circumstances of danger he had used the sign, or ejaculated an appeal to the Cross, admitting thus the virtue of the same; and on one of these occasions, he specifies the place (Sabât al Medâin)

[1] He also objected to the word *Qarîb* (p. 3) as applicable by a Mahometan to a Christian.

where it occurred. Elsewhere he refers to words used by his friend in another discussion about "the Soul." In ridiculing the notion that the name of Mahomet is written on the heavenly throne, the Christian says that none even of his friend's own party held to that conceit. And, again, he apologizes for the warmth of his language by reminding his friend that it was *he* who had begun the controversy.[1]

As regards *Al Kindy* himself, his personality transpires throughout the whole Apology. With a strong attachment to the Nestorian faith, he ever displays a violent aversion from Jews and Magians, on whom, upon all occasions, he bestows the most contumelious epithets. While giving honour to the Hâshimites as chief of the Coreish, he not the less vaunts the superior and kingly dignity of the Beni Kinda, as the blue blood of the Arabs, acknowledged to have been supreme over the whole Peninsula; and he apologizes from his own stand-point as an Ishmaelite, whenever the argument leads him to prefer the lineage of Isaac to that of Ishmael. The repeated assertion of his own learning, experience, and knowledge of mankind and of the various systems of religion and philosophy, is also in keeping with the vein of conscious superiority, tinged with a slight spice of vanity, which runs throughout the Apology.

Add to this that, amidst much that is crude in our view and even illogical, the work is characterized throughout by a singular command of the Arabic language, and that the argument rises at times,—as in the passage on Jehâd and Martyrdom,—to a high pitch of impassioned eloquence, and it must be evident that the writer was a man of remarkable learning and attainments. The Apologist, therefore, could have been no obscure individual. There seems no ground whatever for doubting that he was in reality what he professes naturally and consistently throughout the Apology to be, a scion of the noble Kinda tribe, belonging further to a branch which had clung unwaveringly to their ancestral faith. For the suspicion of a pious fraud in the assumption of that character, there is not,

[1] See pp. 129, 114, 95, and 121.

so far as I can see, any reasonable ground whatever; nor (even if internal evidence admitted the hypothesis) would there have been any sensible advantage in adopting that position.

To sum up, then; I hold that the work may take its stand, on internal evidence, as a composition certainly of the era at which it professes to have been written. Further, there is the strongest probability, amounting almost to certainty, that it is the genuine production of a learned Christian, a man of distinction at the Court of Al Mâmûn, bearing the tribal title of *Al Kindy*. And still further, there is a fair presumption that the Apology was written as a reply to the Appeal prefixed to the Apology, and addressed bonâ fide to his friend by the Moslem, Abdallah Hâshimy, the Caliph's cousin.

There are good grounds for this belief apart altogether from the evidence of Al Bîrûni. But that evidence, as we have seen, is conclusive of the fact that the work was current in the Fourth century, and that it was so under a title corresponding with the account of the authorship as recited in the Preface to the Apology. Al Bîrûni's testimony is, to my mind, chiefly valuable as serving to remove a doubt which must occur to the most casual reader; and that is, whether any one could have dared, at the Metropolis of Islam, to put forth a production written in so fearless and trenchant a spirit against Islam; and whether, this having been done, the obnoxious treatise would not have been immediately suppressed. Religion and the Civil power are, in the Mahometan system, so welded together, that the *læsa Majestas* of the State is ever ready to treat an attack on Islam as high treason of an unpardonable stamp. But the evidence of Al Bîrûni shows that, having survived, our Apology was actually in circulation, in a Mahometan country, a century and a half after the time at which it first appeared. This is almost a greater marvel than that it should even have been written in the first instance; for, under the tolerant sway of the free-thinking Al Mâmûn, that was possible, which a few years later would have been utterly impossible.

And one may be very certain that, when Orthodox views again prevailed, every effort would be made to suppress and exterminate an Apology, obnoxious not only for its attack on the religion of the State, but also for the political sentiments therein advocated as to the divine right of Ali, the usurpation of Abu Bekr, and the manner in which the Coran was compiled. But the work had in all likelihood already so spread during the reign of Al Mâmûn and his immediate Successors (who shared his Motázelite views), that its entire suppression became, no doubt on that account, impossible. And so copies survived, although stealthily, here and there in Mahometan countries. But why this remarkable book was not better known and valued in Christian countries, is very strange, indeed to my mind altogether unaccountable.

Admitting all that has been advanced, it will still remain a question of rare interest who this unknown "Al Kindy, the Christian," was. In a letter from Dr. Steinschneider to Prof. Loth, a suggestion is thrown out which might possibly lead to the identification of our Author. The trace is there given of a *Eustathius al Kindy*, mentioned amóng other Christian and Jewish names by Casiri in his Bibliotheca Arabica, as one of the translators of Aristotle, or copyists of Greek works. May this not have been our Apologist?[1]

Further inqury in this, or some other similar direction, might possibly throw more certain light on the authorship. Other MSS. of the Apology, whether in the East or in our European Libraries, might also with advantage be compared with the printed version to elucidate the purity of the text, and especially of such passages as appear to be imperfect or uncertain in the MSS. from which this edition was printed.[2]

[1] Dr. Steinschneider's letter will be found at page 315 of the Zeitschrift der Morgenländischen Gesellschaft, vol. xxix. The passage referred to in Casiri is as follows: كتاب الالاهيات . . . وهذه الحروف نقلها اسطاث الكندى. Bibliotheca Arab. Hisp. Michaelis Casiri, *Matriti*, 1760 A.D., vol. i. p. 310.

[2] There is the MS. in Paris referred to by de Sacy as No. 257 of the Bibliothèque Orientale. And there is also that mentioned by Steinschneider, No. 112, "*Kindi*, Jacob? Vertheidigung der Christlichen Religion gegen den Islam, in Karschunischen MSS." See his *Polemische und apologetische Literatur in Arabischer Sprache*, Leipzig, 1877, p. 131. In this last, the letter of al Hâshimy (we are told) is given in an abridged form.

The inquiry is not unworthy the attention of the most eminent of our Oriental scholars. The Apology is absolutely unique of its kind. In antiquity, daring, rhetoric, and power, we have nothing in the annals of the Mahometan controversy, at all approaching it. And any research that might throw light upon the origin of the Argument, the circumstances of our Author, the authenticity of the work, and the genuineness of the text handed down to us, must possess not only a literary interest, but in some respects a practical and important bearing on the same struggle which is being waged to-day, as engaged the labours of Abdallah the Hâshimite and Abd al Masîh, Al Kindy, the Christian, in the days of Al Mâmûn.

I have to express my acknowledgments to Prof. Ignatius Guidi of Rome, to Dr. Fritz Hommel of München, and to Dr. Steinschneider of Berlin, for their very kind assistance in the prosecution of this inquiry. To the first, I feel specially grateful for his goodness in copying out for me the entire controversy in which Abu Yûsuf al Kindy appears as an opponent of the doctrine of the Trinity.

THE APOLOGY OF AL KINDY

IN REPLY TO THE

LETTER OF ABDALLAH THE HÂSHIMITE.

Letter of THE HÂSHIMITE to Al Kindy (pp. 2-23).

THE letter of the Mahometan Advocate opens with the salutation of peace and mercy. This, though unusual with Mahometans when addressing Infidels, he justifies by the example of the Prophet, who made no difference, as to his style of address, between *Zimmies* (protected Jews and Christians) and true Believers.[1] He then speaks of the esteem in which Al Kindy was held by the Caliph, his cousin, and of his own warm regard for him. He dwells on his Friend's noble birth, and expresses admiration for his distinguished piety, culture and learning. It was in full accord with the teaching of the Prophet, that he now invited him to embrace Islam, and discuss in a kindly and gracious spirit the merits of their respective creeds.[2] He was himself familiar with Christianity in all its forms. He had read the Jewish and Christian Scriptures, the several Books of which he names in order. He was acquainted with the tenets of the different sects;—the *Melchite*, belonging to the Romish Church; the *Jacobite*, whom he denounces as the most unreasonable of the schismatics; and the *Nestorian*, to which body his Friend was attached, and which he describes in favourable terms;

[1] See, for example, Mahomet's epistle to John ibn Rûbah, the Christian Chief of Aylah, *Life of Mahomet*, p. 457.

[2] He quotes Sura xxix. 46, "Dispute not with the people of the Book otherwise than in the most gracious manner."

for it was the Nestorian branch of the church which was known to Mahomet, and praised by him in the Coran. He was familiar with the rites, prayers, fasts and festivals of the various churches; and had not only visited their Convents and Holy places, but had held discussions with their bishops, priests and learned men. He was not of the vulgar herd, which heaped abuse indiscriminately on all Christians. Conversant with their sects and doctrines, he could appreciate what was good in them. He was thus in a position to call upon his Friend to renounce the errors of his creed, and embrace the grand Catholic faith of Abraham, their common ancestor, with all the attendant blessings of Islam. He then recounts the ordinances and obligations of the Mahometan religion, as Prayer, Fasting, Pilgrimage, Jehâd; dwells on the delights of Paradise that were open to his Friend, and warns him to escape the pains of Hell—supporting his appeal by numerous quotations from the Coran. He had only to embrace the true faith, and he would at once enter on his proper rank and dignity at Court, and share in all the good things of Islam, both in this life and the next. Among the former he mentions the privilege of marrying four wives (liable to divorce if they did not please him) and slave-girls. He closes with an affectionate appeal; and if he should, notwithstanding, choose to hold by the Christian faith, urges him to answer his epistle without fear or favour, under royal guarantee of absolute security.

REPLY OF AL KINDY. Introduction (24, 25).

The Apology of Al Kindy begins with a complimentary address in which he expresses gratitude for the interest shown in his welfare, and an assurance of lasting friendship. He offers a prayer for the long life and prosperity of the Caliph, whose favour he acknowledges with gratitude beyond his power adequately to express. Then follows a petition for help and guidance from Him who had promised that when his servants were brought before kings and governors, it should be given them in that self-same hour what they speak, etc. (quoting Matthew x. 18, 19).

The first section is devoted to a defence of the doctrine of the Trinity, in which the argument is, to our apprehension, often weak and far-fetched. His Friend had invited him to embrace the Catholic, or *Hanyfite*, faith of Abraham, their common father. Our Apologist answers that the Hanyfite faith was in reality the idolatrous religion of the Sabeans, which the Patriarch professed before his conversion to the worship of the One true God. "Which of these two religions of Abraham," he asks, "am I to adopt? If it be the Unity, I reply that the revelation thereof made to Abraham was inherited by Isaac, not by Ishmael, and descended in the line not of the Arabs, but of the Israelites; and it is for them, and not for you, to invite me to the same." After adducing certain metaphysical arguments in favour of the Trinity, he quotes largely from the books of the Old Testament to show that the mystery, though not fully unfolded until the advent of Christ, was plainly fore-shadowed in the Jewish Scriptures. He asserts that the Trinity, as well as the Sonship of the Messiah, are misrepresented in the Coran, and that the notion of a Female element in the Godhead was borrowed by Mahomet from the Jews. He denies that, as stated in the Coran, Christians hold that "God is one of Three," or that "there are three Gods,"—an accusation resting on the heretical dogmas of sects, like the Marcionites, "ignorant dogs," who did not deserve even the name of Christian; and he appeals to his Friend's intimate knowledge to bear him out in his assertion of the true doctrine held by the Church, namely, that there is "One God in three Persons."

The Trinity (25-41).

Our Author is here profuse in quotation from the Old Testament. For example, he refers to the substitution of the Ram for Isaac; the revelation of Jehovah as *I am that I am;* "the God of Abraham, of Isaac, and of Jacob"; the use of the plural number in such passages as, "Let Us go down," which he argues was, according to Hebrew usage, not honorific, but based on the mystery of trinity in unity; the three Angels who visited Abraham; "The

Lord thy God is One Lord;" "*God* made the heavens, by his *Word*, and his *Breath*" (Ps. xxxiii. 6); the Tersanctus of Isaiah, etc. Our Apologist "could rain down showers of similar evidence, if it were not to make his book prolix and wearisome."[1]

Our Author now addresses himself to his Friend's appeal.

Mahomet's prophetic claim a proper subject for discussion (41).

Of the person of Mahomet, connected as Al Hâshimy was by descent with that illustrious personage, he would not say one offensive word.[2] But his claim to be a prophet stood on different ground, and was open to challenge. The summons to believe, coming from any but a tyrant, must be based on reason sufficient to carry conviction. He would therefore discuss the Prophet's career from beginning to end. It was a worthy controversy, in which party spirit and bigotry might well be put aside.

There follows a brief summary of the Prophet's career.

Brief outline of Mahomet's life (42, 43).

In early life an orphan, and an idolator, he was raised to affluence by his marriage with Khadîja. He then sought to reform his people by claiming to be their leader; but, failing in this, because of their pride and tyranny, he assumed the prophetic office, and persuaded the Arabs to accept his teaching,—an ignorant and debased race, who knew neither the beginning nor the issue of the path on which they were entering. He gained them over by yielding to their national love of raids and forays,—and it was

[1] The reasoning is sometimes curious, as in the recognition of three Persons in "the God of Abraham, the God of Isaac, and the God of Jacob." Among the passages with the plural number is that from the Book of Daniel, "God speaks to thee, O king, saying, *To thee* WE *speak, O Nebuchadnezzar*,"—not "I *speak*,"—an expression which I do not trace. Many of Al Kindy's arguments will hardly carry conviction, especially the metaphysical, though these were probably cast in a polemical mould attractive at the time. But the only passage as to the propriety of circulating or translating which I have doubts, is that in which he asserts the *Hanyfite* religion of Abraham to have been, not the Catholic faith of the Unity (as is clearly intended in the Coran), but Sabean idolatry. To support this view, our Author twists texts of the Coran, as where Mahomet is commanded to say, "I am the *first* Moslem." Mahometan readers will with reason object to such misrepresentation of their Scripture.

[2] Our Author never speaks of the Prophet by name, but generally as thy *Master* (Sâhib).

one of these attacks on a caravan belonging to Abu Jahl which led to the Prophet's abandoning Mecca with forty followers. He took refuge in Medina, a poor town inhabited mostly by Jews; and people's eyes were first opened to his true character by the unjust occupation of a plot of land belonging to two orphan children, whereon to build a Mosque.[1]

Warlike and plundering expeditions (44-47).

The next section is devoted to the plundering and warlike expeditions which issued from Medina. The first three, commanded by Companions of the Prophet, are dwelt upon with considerable power. Hamza, sent out with thirty followers, met Abu Jahl at Alîs with three hundred; and, fearing to attack him, retired. Compare this, says Al Kindy, with the aid given by God to Joshua in the conquest of the Promised Land; then one chased a thousand, and two put ten thousand to flight. When Hamza, a believer and follower of Mahomet, gave place to Abu Jahl, the worshipper of idols, where was the Divine help, and where the assistant Angels? The captain of the Lord's host appeared to Joshua before Jericho; and the walls of the city fell down at the blast of the Jewish horns. What parallel can Islam show to that? The next affair was under Abu Obêida, who with seventy men went to Batn Râbigh, to attack Abu Sofiân with two hundred: but no Gabriel appeared to his aid, and he returned empty-handed from the bootless march. How different this from Moses, to whose aid, as the Moslems themselves tell us, Gabriel came and destroyed Pharaoh with his 400,000 followers in the depths of the sea. The third time, Sád was despatched with twenty men to intercept a caravan at Kharrâr; but it had passed a day before, and Mahomet had not known of it. If Mahomet had been a true prophet, he had not thus been left in ignorance; for it is the sign of a true prophet to unfold the unseen, even as Samuel told Saul

Josh. v. vi.

1 Sam. ix.

[1] This short summary is not only confused, but in some points erroneous, as the notice of Abu Jahl, which is misplaced, and the calumny as to the orphans' plot of ground.—See *Life of Mahomet*, p. 181.

of his father's asses being found. Our Saviour said that Matt. xviii. 16. out of the mouth of two or three witnesses, every word would be established; and here, says Al Kindy, are three convincing evidences.[1]

The first three expeditions conducted by Mahomet in person were equally unfortunate, for he missed his plunder and retired crest-fallen. "Judge now for thyself," our Author says, "whether Mahomet could have been a prophet as thou sayest. And what concern have prophets with plunder and pillage? Why did he not leave raids and forays to brigands and highwaymen? Tell me, wherein the difference lies between thy Master and Bâbek Khurramy, whose insurrection hath caused such grief to our lord the Commander of the Faithful, and disaster to mankind at large?[2] I know well that thou canst not answer this. And so it continued all through thy Master's life, even until he died. If a caravan was weak, he attacked it, plundering and slaughtering; but if strong, he fell back and fled. There were nine-and-twenty campaigns in which thy Master engaged in person, besides minor raids and night attacks, and nine pitched battles. Other expeditions were led by his Companions."

Assassinations by Mahomet's command (47-48).

"Still stranger and more flagrant was the commission given by thy Master to assassinate certain persons obnoxious to him. Thus Ibn Rawâha was despatched against Oseir ibn Zârim the Jew, whom he slew by guile; and Ibn Omeir was sent to make away with Abu Afek, also a Jew. This last was an aged man, decrepit and helpless, whom Ibn Omeir perfidiously stabbed to death while asleep at night upon his bed, because he had spoken despitefully of thy

[1] The passages from Scripture, it will be understood, are generally quoted by our Apologist *in extenso*.

[2] Bâbek *Khurramy* (the *festive* or *jovial*) raised the standard of rebellion in Persia about the year 202 A.H. In 212 he carried his conquests into Mesopotamia, and in 214 (just about the time our Apology was written, or shortly before) he annihilated an entire imperial army. He continued the rebellion, with great excesses and cruelty, for twenty years; and it was not till 222 A.H. that he was overthrown and killed. In the course of his insurrection he is said to have slain 250,000 men and six generals. See *Weil's Geschichte der Chalifen*, iii. 301; and *Sale's Koran*, Prel. Discourse, vol. i. p. 213. The terror of his name at the era of the Apology makes the illustration particularly apt.

Master. Tell me, now, I pray thee, whether thou hast anywhere heard or read of so unjustifiable an act; hath any revelation ever sanctioned it; and what kind of ordinance is this, to slay a man simply for speaking words of blame? Had this aged man done anything worthy at all of death, much less of being assassinated unawares? If he spake the truth, should he have been slain for the same? And if he lied, still even for that, one is not to be put to death, but rather chastised that he may refrain therefrom. My Friend, thou well knowest (the Lord be gracious unto thee!) how that it is unlawful to disturb a bird resting in its little nest by night; how much more to slay a man, sleeping securely in his bed, and that for only speaking words of blame! Is this aught but murder? I find not that such an act is justified either by the law of God, of reason, or of nature. Nay, by my life! it is but the old work of Satan towards Adam and his race, ever since he wrought his fall. And how consisteth all this with the saying of thine (the Lord guide thee aright, my Friend!) that thy Master "was sent a Blessing and a Mercy to all mankind."[1]

Other warlike passages (48, 49).

Al Kindy now adverts to one or two other warlike passages in the Prophet's life. Abdallah ibn Jahsh, having been sent towards Mecca with a small party of scouts, attacked a caravan from Yemen, killed the leader, and carried off the spoil to Medina, where Mahomet, after appropriating the royal Fifth, gave over the remainder to the captors. The justice of this proceeding was much canvassed by the citizens of Medina at the time, and our Author leaves it to his Friend to draw his own conclusion.[2]

Expatriation of the Beni Caynocâa.

Equally unjustifiable was the treatment of the Beni Caynocâa, a Jewish tribe on the outskirts of Medina, who without any fault, or colourable excuse, were besieged and forced to surrender at discretion. Abdallah ibn Obey, their ally, pleaded for

[1] For these assassinations, see *Life of Mahomet*, pp. 249 and 362.
[2] *Ibid.* p. 216.

them: at his intercession Mahomet spared their lives; but banishing them to Syria, he laid hold of their property and distributed it among his Companions.[1] "I would (says Al Kindy) that I knew how thy Master reconciled it to his conscience to seize the goods of a people that had not injured him, and with whom there was no ground of quarrel, excepting that he wished to reduce their power, and that they were very rich. Such is not the wont of prophets, nor, indeed, of any that believe in God and in the Last day. I could produce many like things, but that it would weary the reader; and what I have said sufficeth as a sample. But I must say a word as to what

Disaster at Ohod.

befell thy Master on the field of Ohod, when his lower front tooth on the right side was broken, his lip split open, and his cheek and temple gashed, at the hands of Otba; and also what befell Talha, who lost several of his fingers in warding off the sword brandished by Ibn Camea over the Prophet's head.[2] With this compare what our Lord, the Saviour of the world, did, when one of his followers had his ear cut off, and the Messiah put it back in its place, whole even as the other. Now if, when that happened to Talha, thy Master, in whose defence he lost his fingers, had restored them and made the hand whole, that indeed had been the sign of a true prophet. But where were the Angels that they did not come to his help, and save him from having his tooth broken, his lip gashed, and his face covered with blood;—he the Prophet of prophets, the Elect of the elect, the Messenger of the Lord? Where were they, that they did not save him as they delivered the prophets of old—Elijah from the followers of King Ahab; Daniel from the lion of Darius; Ananias and his brethren, the godly youths, from the furnace of Nebuchadnezzar, and other prophets and holy men of God? And yet (as ye hold) Adam and all mankind were created solely on behalf of this thy Master, whose name is also written on the Throne of God!

[1] *Life of Mahomet*, p. 250. [2] *Ibid*, p. 270.

"I turn to another subject. Now, we say that the bent of thy Master's life doth not answer to the boast that he 'was sent a Mercy and Blessing to the human race.' On the contrary, his chief object and concern was to take beautiful women to wife; to attack surrounding tribes, slay and plunder them, and carry off their females for concubines. His chief delights were, by his own confession, sweet scents and women—strange proofs these of the prophetic claim![1] His amour with Zeinab wife of Zeid, I am averse from noticing out of respect for this my book;—excepting only that I will quote the passage which he himself gave forth as having come down from heaven in this matter:

> And when thou saidst to him on whom God had bestowed favour, *Keep thy wife to thyself and fear God;* and thou concealedst in thy mind what God was minded to make known, and thou fearedst man,—whereas God is more worthy that thou shouldst fear him. And when Zeid had fulfilled her divorce, WE joined thee in marriage unto her, that there might be no offence chargeable to Believers in marrying the wives of their adopted sons, after they have fulfilled their divorce; and the command of God is to be fulfilled. There is no offence chargeable to the Prophet in that which God hath enjoined upon him, according to the ordinance of God in respect of those that preceded him;—and the command of God is a predestined decree.—Sura xxxiii. 36, 37.[2]

"This specimen will suffice for men of understanding."

Ayesha's misadventure.

Next is introduced the story of Ayesha's night adventure with Safwân, which created a great scandal at Medina, and made Mahomet suspicious of his favourite wife;—whereupon Ali addressed him in the same sense, ending with these words: *O Prophet of God! the Lord hath not straitened thee in this matter, and there are many other women besides her.* "But he would not be persuaded, because of his uxorious fondness of Ayesha, whom

[1] There is an objectionable passage here, p. 50, lines 4 and 5, which (however much it may add point to the passage) I would omit in the translation. It is besides based on a weak tradition.

[2] See *Life of Mahomet*, p. 302.

only he married a maiden, and who being young and bewitching had possession of his heart (and this was the cause of the enmity between Ali and Ayesha all their life long), so that in the end he promulgated a revelation of her innocence, in Sura Nûr—*Verily they that slander married women,* etc. The story is notorious and needeth from me no further application."[1]

Then follows an enumeration of Mahomet's wives, with remarks on certain of them. Omm Salma, our Author tells us, was of a jealous temperament, and wished to avoid the honour of the prophet's hand by the excuse that she had several children to tend; whereupon Mahomet engaged to bring them up, but in this he deceived her, for he never fulfilled the promise.[2] Of Zeinab he relates that after Mahomet had thrice sent her portion of meat she flung it back in his face, whereupon he swore that he would not go near his wives for a whole month; but not having patience to wait till the end, he approached them after nine-and-twenty days.[3] Safia, the Jewess, was taught by the prophet, when upbraided by her sister-wives, to answer, saying, *Aaron is my father, Moses my uncle, and Mahomet my husband.* Muleika, of the Kinda tribe, when solicited by the prophet to be his wife, exclaimed, *What! shall Muleika give herself to a merchantman?*[4] The remaining wives are little more than mentioned by name; in all he had fifteen wives and two slave-girls. "Paul, the Apostle, said, *He that hath a wife, his object is how he may please her,* etc.; and he spake the truth, for a man is ever occupied with what may please his wife. Our Saviour

Wives of Mahomet.

1 Cor. vii. 32, 33.

[1] *Life of Mahomet*, p. 313.

[2] Al Kindy therefore calls her "the Deceived." Her excuse and the prophet's promise are certainly mentioned in tradition; but I do not recollect anything to show that in not himself bringing up the children, or adopting them as his own, Mahomet "deceived" the lady. See *Life of Mahomet*, p. 300.

[3] The cause of Mahomet's oath is ordinarily attributed to a worse scandal. *Ibid*, p. 442.

[4] A stroke of our Author's at the superiority of the kingly Kinda lineage over the Coreish, who were a tribe of merchantmen. We shall see that he refers to this again.

also said, *No man can serve two masters at one and the same time; he must needs serve one and slight the other.* Now, if it be so that a man cannot serve a single wife and please her without neglecting his Maker, how much more must one have been taken up in seeking to please fifteen wives, besides two that were bond-maids? Add to this that he was all the while engaged in raids and forays and military expeditions, in ordering his troops for the same, in sending out spies, and in planning how to circumvent his enemies, slay their men, take their women captive and plunder their goods. How then could thy Master find leisure from all these cares and pleasures for fasting and prayer, worship, meditation and preparation for the life to come? I am very sure that no prophet in olden times resembled him in these things."

Prophecy an evidence of Divine mission (53-57).

The next section is on prophecy as the evidence of a Divine commission. It is of two kinds. Revelation of the past, accredited by miracles,—as the account by Moses of the creation and ancient history of man. *Second;*—Revelation of the future, accredited by fulfilment, either immediately, as Isaiah's prediction of the destruction of the army of Sennacherib King of Mosul, and the recovery of Hezekiah; or at some future time, as the Promise of the Holy Land, the return of the Captivity, the Coming of the Messiah, His death, and the Scattering of the Jews,—foretold by Isaiah, Jeremiah and Daniel. Such evidence was required of all who claimed the prophetic office, and by the issues of the same they were accepted or rejected. The Messiah, the Saviour of the world, was the greatest of all the prophets. They were servants of the Great God; but he was His beloved Son, and himself the inspirer of the prophets. He knew the unseen. No heart was closed, no secret hidden from him; and He foretold things to come. In proof are quoted prophecies by Jesus regarding the destruction of the Temple, his own decease and the persecutions that should follow. He acquainted His disciples with the death of Lazarus, and then raised

Matthew xxiv. 1, 2.

him to life again. Our Author concludes with Peter's threefold denial as foretold by our Saviour, and his bitter sorrow for the same.

Wanting in the case of Mahomet (57).

"Now, tell me," he proceeds, "what thing thy Master foretold, or made known, in virtue of which thou holdest him to be a prophet. If thou sayest that he made known to us the history of the prophets that went before him, as of Noah, Abraham, Isaac, Jacob, Moses, the Messiah, and others,—I have a ready answer; namely, that he told us what we knew already, and even our very children read at school. And if thou wilt make mention of such other narratives, as of Ad and Thamûd, of Sâlih and his Camel, of the Elephant and the like, I reply that these are witless fables, and old wives' tales, such as we Arabs hear night and day, and are no proof whatever of a Divine mission. And so the evidence of the past falleth to the ground. And if thou sayest that he foretold what was to happen in the future, it behoveth thee to give instances of the same; for over 200 years have elapsed since his time, and surely something of what he foretold must have come to pass ere this. But thou knowest, and we all know, that thy Master never uttered a single prophecy; and so the other condition also faileth."

Miracles disavowed by Mahomet (58).

Sura xvii. 60.

"Such being the case, let us see whether there is any sign of the second kind of evidence, to wit, of miracles. Now, Mahomet himself hath told us plainly that it was said to him (by the Almighty), *Nothing hindered* Us *from sending thee with Miracles, but that those of old time gave them the lie;* that is to say, 'If it had not been that thy people would have called them impostures, even as those of old did, we should have bestowed on thee the gift of Miracles.' Now, by my life, what, according to all the rules of logic, could be a more conclusive answer! Thou knowest (the Lord guide thee!), and all they that hear my Apology know, that thy Master herein disclaimed miracles as a proof of his mission, because he had not the power of showing them; and it is not for an impartial man like thee to turn aside from the truth.

Saracen conquest of Persia no proper evidence (58, 59).

"If thou claimest, as a proof of his mission, that thy Master and his Companions, notwithstanding they were few and weak, trampled under foot the mighty kingdom of Persia, with all its resources, armies, and munitions of war, then we answer thee in the words of the Lord to the children of Israel, 'Not because the Lord loved you above all nations, hath he given you the victory over the Amorites and Perizzites so that ye have slain them, ravaged their lands and inherited their cities, but because of the wickedness of these nations, and the greatness of their iniquity, hath he given you the victory over them.'[1] Thus He treated even Jerusalem, the city of His choice, the abode of His prophets, the scene of great wonders and miracles, whence praise and worship ascended day and night, the spot where prayer was wont to be answered, the seat of blessing from above;—when her citizens rebelled against Him, set up other gods, denied His signs and forgat His mercies, thinking they had gotten them by the might of their own hand,—then the Lord gave up Jerusalem into the power of that wickedest of mankind, Nebuchadnezzar, the idolator, who slew the inhabitants thereof, even that chosen race, and carried them away captive and their children, and destroyed the House called by His own name, and took away the holy vessels that were therein to the abominable Babylon for the service of idols. Now, wilt thou say that Nebuchadnezzar, in that he stormed the Holy city, and inflicted these calamities upon it, was a prophet, because of all this? Even thus is the case of thy Master and his followers with this great kingdom of Persia. For the people were all Magians, wicked and abominable, the dregs of nations, and the vilest of mankind. They worshipped the Sun and Fire; they took to wife their own daughters, sisters, and mothers; they rebelled

[1] Paraphrased from Deut. ix. 4, 5.

against the truth, and exalted themselves beyond measure; in their heathenism they attributed Divinity to those whom the Lord hath not made to be gods; they abused His gifts and corrupted the land, and thought that their prosperity was verily the work of their own wisdom and might. Wherefore the Lord gave them into the hands of those that ravaged their land, slew their men, destroyed their habitations, made their families captive, and robbed their goods, so that there remained not a woman amongst them but was seized as a concubine, nor one of their children but was led away into slavery. For thus doth the Lord judge an ungodly people."

Miracles disclaimed in the Coran (60).

Returning to the excuse of Mahomet that he was not gifted with miracles, lest his people, as of old, should call them impostures, our Author repeats,—"By my life! a strange reason to offer to any man of sense. Allow that the Jews aforetime did give the lie to the miracles of their prophets, and rejected them, what then? As to the Arab tribes they could never have given them the lie, seeing that no prophet had arisen amongst them before, nor any Apostle in Arabia, whether with miracles or without them. Doubtless had thy Master shown them anything like a miracle, they would have attested the same, and not given it the lie; for do we not see that multitudes of these same Arabs did accept his ministry, although they saw no miracles, neither heard of any wonderful work? But thou well knowest (the Lord preserve thee!) that this argument will not stand inquiry."

Fabulous tales handed down by tradition (60-64).

"If now, leaving the testimony of the Coran, we turn to fables and stories, then we get to such fond tales as that of the Wolf which stood howling before Mahomet; whereupon he turned to his Companions saying that this wolf was a deputation from the Beast of the forests:—'Wherefore if ye will (continued he) let us impose upon it certain conditions which they shall not transgress; or if ye will we shall let it go free.' They answered that they did not care to impose conditions; then Mahomet made signs to it with his three fingers, whereupon it turned and went away. Wonderful! (proceeding in a strain of irony) that Mahomet should understand the inarticulate bark of a wolf! Suppose he had said, *This wolf is a messenger from the Almighty to me,* could any one have gainsaid it? Such tales, my brother, are meant only for ignorant people innocent of reason and the laws of evidence." Another story of a wolf speaking to one of the Companions (strange that both miracles should be in connection with an animal called in the Scriptures "ravening") he treats with equal contempt. Such conceits were not for sensible men, and there was no need to dwell longer on them. He dismisses with similar scorn the legend of the bull that spoke; the goat whose empty udders swelled when touched by Mahomet; and the tree which advanced at his call, ploughing up the ground—a tradition rejected even by intelligent Moslems. More space is given to the miracle of the *Roasted shoulder of mutton* sent to the Prophet by Zeinab the Jewess, which told him that it was poisoned, and of which Bishr ate and died thereof. "Either Mahomet alone heard the shoulder speak, and then why did he conceal the matter, and not prevent Bishr (a chosen guest) from eating? or the whole company heard it, and then Bishr himself would surely have refrained. There is no escape from the dilemma. Or, Bishr ate on, perhaps, secure in the company of a prophet whom the Lord heard alway, and answered his prayers. Why then did not thy Master pray to his Lord, as the prophets of old who interceded and the dead were raised to life again; even as Elias raised the widow's son, and his disciple Elisha the son of the Shunamite. And after his death, virtue yet remained in the bones of Elisha, so that a dead man placed upon the same revived and stood upon his feet. Thou knowest that this is true, for it is in the Scripture, as thou mayest read in the Book of Kings. There is no difference in the text between the Jews and Christians; for though we differ in religion we agree in the truth of this. Now, why, when Bishr did eat, was the poison not made harmless? Then had

2 Kings xii. 21.

it been a sign of thy Master's prophetic office: for prophets and holy men of old were shielded by the Lord from calamities incident to unbelief,—according to the promise of our Lord to his disciples in the holy Gospel, which was fulfilled to them, in that He said, *If ye drink deadly poison, it shall not hurt you;* that is to say, when ye put forth your claim that men may listen to the Gospel, this shall come to pass. And they did so, and published their message by means of these miracles. And thus great and powerful kings and philosophers and learned men and judges of the earth hearkened unto them, without the lash or rod, with neither sword nor spear, nor the advantages of birth or helpers—with no wisdom of this world or eloquence or power of language or subtlety of reason, with no worldly inducement nor any relaxation of the moral law, but simply at the voice of truth enforced by miracles beyond the power of man to show.[1] And so there came over to them the kings and great ones of the earth; and the philosophers abandoned their systems, and with all their wisdom and learning betook them to a saintly life, giving up the delights of this world and their established usages, and became followers of a company of poor men, fishers and publicans, who had neither name nor rank, or any claim other than that they were obedient to the command of the Messiah,—he that gave them the power to do such wonderful works. Now these, if ye will, (the Lord guide thee, my friend!) are proofs of a Divine mission, not such silly things as are told of thy Master, in which there is no reality. As for the miracle of the pitcher into which they say he thrust his hand, and forthwith there issued water, so that they drank therefrom, they and their beasts—the account comes from Mohammed ibn Ishâc (and) Zohri,[2] and the authority is insufficient; for even the traditionists themselves are not at one about the truth of it. Thus the historical evidence altogether fails,

[1] In all this a direct contrast is intended with the spread of Islam.

[2] The text reads as if *Zohri* were a title of Ibn Ishâc; probably a typographical mistake, as Zohri flourished fifty years earlier—*Life of Mahomet*, p. 603. For the incident referred to see *Ibid*, p. 369.

and the claim must be abandoned. Instead of miracles, the claim of thy Master was enforced simply by the sword. Whosoever hesitated to acknowledge him a prophet sent by God, was slain, or spared only on payment of tribute, as the price of his unbelief.

Mahomet warned his people not to believe such lying tales (64).

"Finally, what could be more conclusive proof, if thou wilt judge impartially (the Lord guide thee!), than this, that thy Master himself cut away the ground from all such tales as are told of him, in that he said openly and plainly, 'There 'hath been no prophet, but his people have told 'lies about him; and I am no exception that my people 'should not tell lies about me. Wherefore, whensoever ye 'shall hear aught about me, then turn to the book which 'I have left with you; and if it conform thereto, and there 'be mention of the same in it, then it is true that I said 'or did what is related of me; but if there be no mention 'of it in the book, then I am free therefrom, and that which 'is related of me is a lie, and I neither said nor did it.' Wherefore see, my friend, and judge, whether those stories which thy people tell are to be found at all in the book of the Coran; if there be any mention of them, or any trace, therein, then, by my life! I will confess that it is true, and that thy Master did the same. Otherwise he is absolved from these fictions, and they are goundless lying tales for which he is not in any wise responsible.

Tradition that Mahomet would rise again after three days (64).

"Of the same kind, but much worse is the tradition regarding thy Master's obsequies. He desired (so the story runs) that he should not be buried for three days, seeing that the Lord would raise him to Heaven even as He raised our Saviour Christ, because he was too honourable to be left longer upon the earth. So after he died they refrained till the fourth day, when, forced by the progress of decay, they buried him."[1]

[1] Some irrelevant observations follow as to the part taken by Aly and Abbâs in the funeral obsequies. Parts of the work have here somewhat the appearance of dislocation. The object of introducing the passage is apparently to show how misleading the traditions of the Prophet's life may be.

"After his decease, there remained not one of thy Master's followers that did not apostatize, saving only a small company of his Companions and kinsfolk, who were ambitious of succeeding to the government. Here Abu Bekr displayed marvellous skill, energy and address, so that the power fell into his hands. Aly was exceedingly angry thereat; and people resorted to him, not doubting that he would succeed; but the reins were snatched from his hands, from love of the world and lust of power.[1] But Abu Bekr persevered, until the apostate tribes were all brought back to their allegiance, some by kindly treatment, persuasion and craft, some through fear and terror of the sword, and others by the prospect of power and wealth and the lusts and pleasures of this life. And so it came to pass that they were all in the end converted outwardly, and not from inward conviction."

APOSTACY of the Arabs (65).

To establish this point, our Apologist quotes a speech delivered at an assembly of his courtiers by the Caliph in which he likens the hypocritical conversion of the Magians, Jews and Christians of his own day, to that of the Jews and hypocrites in the time of Mahomet, and justifies his own forbearance by the Prophet's example, and the worldly inducements by which the apostates were reclaimed.[2]

Speech of Al-Mámûn, showing how the Apostates were reclaimed by worldly inducements (66).

The objection is here anticipated that if Moses and Joshua attacked and slew the Canaanites, took their families captive, and ravaged their land, similar acts should not be charged against Mahomet as a fault. But the slaughter of the Canaanites, Al Kindy replies, was a chastisement from heaven, and the commission to inflict the same was ratified by miracles, which he recounts and which he reminds his Friend that both Jews and Christians, though hostile in other respects, agree in attesting. "Show me," he proceeds, "any the slightest

Mahomet showed no miracles, like Moses and Joshua, to warrant resort to the sword (68–70).

[1] All this (which is altogether opposed to historical evidence) is in accord with the Alyite current that ran strong at Al Mâmûn's court.

[2] This has been given *in extenso* in the Preliminary Essay, p. xii.

proof or sign of a wonderful work done by thy Master to certify his mission, and to prove that what he did in slaughter and rapine was, like the other, by Divine command. I know thou canst not. And so it behoveth thee not (the Lord direct thee!) to blame or injure those who deny that the Lord sent thy Master as an Apostle with the commission to impose his religion by the sword, and hold him to have been an adventurer seeking his own ends and aided therein by his kinsfolk, clan, and fellow-citizens. If any reject the claim of such a one, they are not justly to be blamed; but rather, if judged impartially, to be praised and commended for searching out the truth. To bolster up fallacies and falsehoods consisteth neither with reason nor justice. These are the weapons of the Jews and heathen, who deal in lies like their father the Devil, even as Jesus Christ our Saviour hath shown in the holy Gospel.

Al Kindy invites his Friend to consider the claims of Jesus Christ based on miracles (70, 71).

"And now, as to thine invitation, suppose I should accept it without reason or evidence, wouldest thou regard that as the course of rectitude? I trow not. And judge, my Friend, how should I do this, and my Lord the Messiah hath said in the holy Gospel, *All the prophets have prophesied until the time of my coming;* that is, at the era of my appearance, the prophetic office ceaseth; and whosoever cometh after me claiming to be a prophet, the same is a wolf and a robber, receive him not.[1] Tell me, my good friend, if turning aside from the dying command of my Lord, the Saviour of the world, I should be tempted by the pomps, vanities, and carnal inducements of this life, to accept thy call without proof,—I think not that one like thee, endowed with righteousness and wisdom, would approve a sin so heinous, neither is it possible that one like me could turn aside thereto. Nay, my Friend, rather would I appeal to thy reason, and beseech of thee, casting aside considerations of birth and family, to listen unto me, thy true counsellor and affectionate adviser. Call

[1] Referring possibly to John x. or Acts xx. 29.

to mind what in the holy Gospel, our Lord, the Messiah, saith to His disciples—'Truly many prophets and kings desired to see what ye see and did not see it, and to hear what ye hear and did not hear it.' How canst thou, reading such words, turn therefrom, loving this present life, which swiftly passeth away and disappeareth." The Section on miracles closes here with an eloquent recapitulation of the argument for the truth of Christianity, based on the way in which it spread, not by force, or through any ambitious, sordid, and carnal motives, but simply from choice and conviction, grounded on the incontestable miracles of Christ and His disciples.

THE THREE DISPENSATIONS: Divine, Natural and Satanic (72-75).

Entering now upon a new argument, Al Kindy lays it down as axiomatic that there are but three Dispensations, to one or other of which the religion of Mahomet must belong. *First*, the Divine; *second*, the Natural; and *third*, the Satanic.

Matthew v. 44, 45.

Sura v. 53.

First, the Divine, so called because moulded in the likeness of God himself, it transcends reason, and is more excellent than anything drawn from nature. The same is the Gospel, or dispensation of Grace brought by Jesus Christ, and described in the Coran as "a light and guidance, and a direction to the pious." It is based on Favour, Mercy, and Forgiveness, even as our Saviour commanded us to overcome evil with good, after the example of our Father in heaven. The *second* is the law of reason or nature, summed up by Moses in the text "an eye for an eye," etc.; that is, the law of like for like, returning good for good, and evil for evil, and therein differing altogether from the Gospel which follows the gracious dealing of the Lord with his creatures. The *third* is the kingdom of the Evil One, tyranny, and wrong. Conscious of treading upon delicate ground, Al Kindy here deprecates his friend's displeasure; they were in the heat of conflict, and he could not afford to dispense with any of those spiritual weapons from which he hoped for victory. Nor would it be just to blame him, for he had borne patiently things equally severe from the other side. Beginning with a prayer that God would guide his Friend, he asks him which of the three was his Master's creed. "If thou sayest, 'The Divine'; I reply, that our Lord the Christ, 600 years before, revealed the same Dispensation; ever since His Ascension unto the present day, His followers have observed it; and they will follow the same to the end of time. Moreover, I perceive not that thy fellows know aught concerning this law of Grace and Mercy, and as little did they act upon it in thy Master's day. If thou sayest, 'the Natural law' of reason and justice, that too was revealed aforetime by Moses, and is contained in the Tourât; and being there, clear as the sun-beam, it were piracy and falsehood, if any other claimed to be the author of the same. There remaineth the third, the law of Satan, wrong-doing and evil. Now look (the Lord guide thee!) with an eye that shall not deflect from the right, and see who it is that taketh his stand on this dispensation, seeketh help therefrom, and practiseth its principles. And if not this, then tell me what new Dispensation thy Master came with, and what law other than this he revealed, that I may embrace the same, if it be worthy of acceptance; for I will not refuse the truth from whatsoever quarter it may come. Perchance thou wilt say that thy Master combined the two former dispensations both together, to wit, the rule of the Messiah and the rule of Moses—following up the law of 'Life for life, eye for eye, tooth for tooth, nose for nose, etc.,' with the command of our Lord 'but if ye forgive, it is nigher unto piety.' But thou well knowest that the two being contradictory, will not consist together,—as if one were to say that a man was standing and sitting, blind and seeing, healthy and diseased, at one and the same time; and I think not that thou wouldest admit so untenable a claim. Besides, this amalgamated creed would have been fetched from two separate sources, the Gospel, and the Tourât. And supposing thou wert to say, 'I adopt both these Dispensations'; I think not that the professors of either would acknowledge thee;

Sura v. 53. Sura ii. 238; v. 9.

for they have inherited their respective creeds and hold the same in their hands intact; and would reply that it was simple plagiarism. Nay rather, do thou show us something of thine own, which is in thy hands, and not in ours, but new; and we shall then acknowledge thee to be true and just. Ah, is it not because thou takest refuge in the third, and seeketh help therefrom, however much thou mayest disclaim it? For I wot not that thou wouldest consent to hold thy Master as a mere follower of Moses and the Messiah,—seeing that thou claimest for him a position so exalted that had it not been for him neither Adam nor the world would have taken shape. And that thy Master showed no miracle (as he himself disclaimed the power), why was it but because there remained no fourth dispensation? Now if there are but three, and Moses and the Messiah came with two, what is there left for thy Master but the third? I know not which of these answers I am to choose. I pray thee, my Friend, be honest with thyself, and evade not the question, for that were against the conditions of this controversy; seeing that Religion is not one of those matters which men of sense and understanding can refrain from probing and discussing, or neglect to test by right principle. The Lord lead thee graciously to the Truth, and strengthen thee to abandon the False."

THE CORAN as an evidence of Mahomet's Mission (75-90).

"We come now to what thou regardest as thy stronghold, to wit, the Book which is in thy hands. Thine argument is that the narratives therein of the prophets and the Messiah prove that it was revealed by God, because thy Master was unlearned, and could have had no knowledge of the same excepting by way of inspiration. Again, thou sayest that 'neither man nor genius could produce the like thereof'; and, 'If ye be in doubt as to that which We have revealed unto Our servant, then bring a Sura the like thereof, and call your witnesses other than the Lord, if ye be true men.' And, yet again, 'If We had sent down this Coran unto a mountain, thou

Sura ii. 23.

Sura lix. 21.

wouldest have seen it humbling itself, and cleaving asunder, from fear of the Lord'; and the like effusions. This in thy view is the main evidence of thy Master's claim, ranking with the miracle of the Red Sea, the Staying of the Sun, the Raising of the Dead, and other wonderful works by the prophets of old and the Messiah. And, by my life! this argument hath deceived many. But it is a weak and hollow subterfuge. The answer is near at hand, and not far off, as I will show thee. The disclosure may be bitter, but it will be wholesome in the end." He then proceeds to give a lengthy account of the origin of the Coran.[1] His story in short is this. "Sergius, a Nestorian monk, was excommunicated for a certain offence. To expiate it, he set out on a mission to Arabia, and reached Mecca, which he found inhabited by Jews and idolators. There he met Mahomet, with whom he had intimate converse, and persuaded him, after being instructed in the faith of Nestorius, to abandon heathenism, and become his disciple. This, while it excited the hatred of the Jews, was the reason of the favourable mention of the Christians in the Coran, to wit, that 'they are the nighest Sura v. 91.
'unto believers in friendship; and that because there are 'amongst them priests and monks, and because they are not 'haughty.' And so the matter prospered, and the Christian faith was near to being adopted, when Sergius died. Thereupon two Jewish Doctors, Abdallah and Kab, seized the opportunity, and ingratiated themselves with thy Master, professing deceitfully to share his views and be his followers. Thus they concealed their object and bided their time. Then upon the Prophet's death, when Aly kept aloof and refused to swear allegiance to Abu Bekr, the two Jews sought him out, and tried to persuade him to assume the prophetic office, for which they declared him fit, and promised to instruct him, as Sergius had instructed Mahomet.

[1] This long digression about the Coran is strongly coloured by Abbasside and Alyite tradition. Much of it is mere romance, resting on no historical evidence whatever. But it was no doubt the kind of talk popular at the Court of Al Mâmûn (where any argument impugning the eternity of the Coran, would be well received); and, indeed, our Author here and there implies as much.

Aly, yet young and inexperienced, listened to them, and was instructed secretly.[1] Before they had fully gained their object, Abu Bekr heard of it and sent for Aly, who finding opposition useless, abandoned his ambitious claim. But the Jews had already succeeded in tampering with the text which Mahomet left in Aly's hands, that namely which was based upon the Gospel. It was then that these Jews interpolated histories from the Old Testament, and portions of the Mosaic law, and introduced such passages as this:—

Sura ii. 113. 'The Christians say that the Jews are founded 'upon nothing, and the Jews say that the Christians are 'founded upon nothing; and yet they read the Book. Thus 'did the ignorant people aforetime speak as they do. Where-'fore the Lord will judge between them in the day of 'the Resurrection as to that concerning which they differ.' Hence also arose inconsistencies in the Coran,—passages proceeding from one source, differing from passages that proceeded from another; as in Chapters, the Bee, the Ant, the Spider. (Suras xvi. xxvii. and xxix.) Now when Aly despaired of succeeding to the Caliphate, he repaired to Abu Bekr forty days (some say six months) after the Prophet's death. As he was swearing allegiance, Abu Bekr asked him, 'O Father of Hasan, what hath delayed thee so long?' He answered, '*I was busy collecting the Book of the Lord*, for the Prophet committed that to me.' Reflect, my Friend, what could have been the meaning of his being busy in collecting the Book of God? Thou knowest how the tyrant Hajjâj 'collected' the leaves of the Coran, and left out much thereof. Ah, deceived one! the Book of God is not 'collected,' nor can any part thereof be lost. Thou, and those of thy persuasion, know and acknowledge all that I have said, for it is taken from traditions of your own in which all of you agree. According to some authorities, the first copy was left with the Coreish, and Aly, when he came to power, ordered it to be taken possession of lest it should be tampered with; and this was the copy

[1] Hardly young and inexperienced, being then over six-and-twenty years.

which was in accord with the Gospel as delivered to Mahomet by Sergius.[1] Now when Aly spake to Abu Bekr, as related above, those about him replied, that there were scraps and pieces of the Coran with them as well as with Aly; and it was agreed to collect the whole together. So they collected various parts from the memory of individuals, (as Sura *Barât*, which they wrote out at the dictation of a certain Arab from the desert,) and other portions from different people, and from the deputations which had visited the Prophet; besides that which was copied out from tablets of stone, and palm leaves, and shoulder bones, and such like. It was not at first collected in a volume, but remained in separate leaves; and so the Jews got what they wanted inserted through the leaves of Aly. Sura ix.

"Then the people fell to variance in their reading. Some read according to the version of Aly (and they follow the same to the present day); some read according to the collection of which we have made mention. Others read according to the reading of the Arab from the desert who in his ignorance made changes and additions. A party read according to the text of Ibn Masûd, following the saying of thy Master,—'Whosoever would read the Coran in its pristine purity and freshness, let him read after Ibn Omm Mabad'; and he used to repeat it over to him once every year, and in the year he died, twice. And, yet again, some read after Obey ibn Kab, following thy Master's word;—'The best Reader amongst you all, is Obey.' Now the readings of Obey and Ibn Masûd are close one to the other.

"Thus when Othmân came to power, and people everywhere differed in their readings, Aly sought grounds of accusation against him, compassing his death.[2] One man would read a verse one way, and another man another way, each saying that his reading was better than his neighbour's,

[1] Our Author tells us that this Sergius was also called by the Companions "Gabriel," and at other times "The faithful Spirit."

[2] The sentence is remarkable, preceding as it does the notice of Othmân's recension, and also as plainly imputing to Aly a design prepense on the life of Othmân.

and contending for the same; and there was change and interpolation, some copies having more and some less. When this was represented to Othmân, and the danger urged of division, strife and apostacy, he thereupon caused to be collected together all the leaves and scraps that he was able, together with what was copied out at the first. But they did not meddle with that which was in the hands of Aly, or of those who followed his reading. Obey was dead by this time. As for Ibn Masûd, they demanded his exemplar, but he refused to give it up, and so Abu Mûsa was appointed governor of Kufa in his room.[1] Then they commanded Zeid ibn Thâbit, and with him Abdallah ibn Abbâs (others say Mohummed, son of Abu Bekr), to revise and correct the text, eliminating all that was corrupt. Now both were young;[2] and they were instructed when they differed on any reading, word, or name, to follow the dialect of the Coreish. On many points they did differ. For instance, Zeid wrote *Tâbûh*, and Ibn Abbâs *Tâbût*. When the recension was completed, four exemplars were written out in large text, and sent one to Mecca, and another to Medîna. The third was despatched to Syria, and is to this day at Malatia (Melitene). The copy at Mecca remained there till the city was stormed by Abu Sarâya (that is, the last time the Káaba was sacked, A.H. 200); he did not carry it away; but it is supposed to have been burned in the conflagration. The Medîna exemplar was lost in the reign of terror, that is, in the days of Yezîd ibn Muâvia. The fourth exemplar was deposited in Kûfa, then the centre of Islam and home of the Companions of the Prophet. People say that this copy is still extant there; but this is not the case, for it was lost in the insurrection of Mukhtâr.[3]

"After what we have related above, Othmân called in all the former leaves and copies, and destroyed them,

[1] The deposition is true, but not the cause here alleged for it.

[2] Our Author is not accurate. At the Hegira, Zeid was eleven, and Abdallah six years of age; so at the era of Othmân's recension they must have been thirty and thirty-five years old, respectively.

[3] Mukhtâr was slain in the rebellion here referred to, A.H. 67.

threatening those who held any portion back; and so only some scattered remains, concealed here and there, survived. Nothing remained to show the discrepancies which are known to have existed. It is said for example that Sura Nûr (xxiv.) used to be longer than Sura Bacr (ii.),[1] and that Sura Ahzâb (xxxiii.) is mutilated and incomplete; so also that there was originally no division between Sura Barât (ix.) and Sura Anfâl (viii.), and accordingly we see that the invariable heading *In the name of God most Merciful,* is wanting in the former. Similar is the case of the two 'Incantation Suras,'[2] of which Ibn Masûd said when they were placed in the Coran: *Add not thereto that which is not therein.* And then there is the speech of Omar delivered from the pulpit (of the Great Mosque at Medîna), 'Let no one say that the *Stoning Verse* is not in the Book of God; for verily I have myself read, *The man and the woman that commit adultery, let them both be stoned to death*; and if it were not that men might say, 'Omar hath added to the Coran that which is not therein,' I would have inserted the same with mine own hand.'[3] Likewise at the close of another address: 'Truly I know not of any one who saith that the Ordinance of temporary marriage (*Al Mutah*) is not in the Book of the Lord, for, indeed, I have myself read it; but it hath fallen out. And verily the Lord will not reward him well that caused it to fall out; for a trust was given, and he fulfilled not the trust of the Lord and of his prophet; and verily much that belonged to the Coran hath thus fallen out.' And yet once more, Omar said: 'The Lord was not minded to deal lightly with mankind, for verily he sent Mahomet with a wide and comprehensive faith.'

"And Obey ibn Kab said that there were two Suras which he used to recite (as part of the Coran:) *Al Canût* and *Al Witr*; in them were these words: 'O Lord, we ask thee for help and pardon and guidance, and we believe in thee

[1] The longest Sura in the Coran.
[2] The last two Suras, of only a line or two each.
[3] See *Life of Mahomet* (1st edition), vol. i. p. xxv.

and put our trust in thee,' and so on to the end of *Al Wetr*. (This he said in respect of the first compilation, no longer extant.)

"Again, as regards the same Ordinance of temporary marriage (al Mutah), Aly caused the passage about it to be entirely excluded. They say that while Caliph, he overheard a man reciting the verse, and had him scourged for the same, and forbade its further repetition. And this was one of the things for which Ayesha reproached Aly after the battle of the Camel when she had retired to the house of Ibn Khalaf (at Bussora); for, among other things, she said that Aly had beaten men in this matter of the Coran, and forbade the repetition of certain passages, and tampered with the text. Moreover, Ibn Masûd retained his exemplar in his own hands, and it was inherited by his posterity, as it is this day; and likewise the collection of Aly hath descended in his family.

"Then followed the business of Hajjâj ibn Yûsuf, who gathered together every single copy he could lay hold of, and caused to be omitted from the text a great many passages. Amongst these, they say, were verses revealed concerning the House Omeyya with the names of certain, and concerning the House of Abbâs also with names. Six copies of the text thus revised were distributed to Egypt, Syria, Medîna, Mecca, Kûfa, and Bussora. After that he called in and destroyed all the preceding copies, even as Othmân had done before him.

"And the result of all this is patent to thee who hast read the Scriptures, and seest how in thy book histories are all jumbled together and intermingled; an evidence that many different hands have been at work therein, and caused discrepancies, adding or cutting out whatever they liked or disliked. Are such, now, the conditions of a Revelation sent down from heaven?

"Furthermore, thy Master was an Arab, living amongst the Bedouins; and before them, and in their language, he laid his lucubrations. Now it is notorious that the Arabs as a nation are incorrigibly heathenish and graceless; how could such a people receive from him the secret of the Lord, or truths proper to be revealed to a prophet? Thou knowest the enmity subsisting between Aly and Abu Bekr, Omar, and Othmân; and each of these entered whatever favoured his own claims, and left out what was otherwise. How, then, can we distinguish between the genuine and the counterfeit? And how about the losses caused by Hajjâj? Thou well knowest what kind of faith that tyrant held in other matters; then how canst thou make him an arbiter as to the Book of God,—a man who never ceased to play into the hands of the Omeyyads whenever he found opportunity. And besides all this, the Jews also had a hand in the business; and foisted in what they thought would further their own seditious and rebellious ends.

"All that I have said (continues Al Kindy, after an affectionate personal appeal) is drawn from your own authorities; and no argument have I advanced but what is based on evidence accepted by yourselves. And in proof thereof, we have the Coran itself, which is a confused heap with neither system nor order. The sense moreover consisteth not with itself; but throughout one passage is contradicted by another. Now, what could betray greater ignorance than to bring forward such a book as an evidence of Apostleship, and to put it on a par with the miracles of Moses and Jesus! Surely no one with a grain of sense would dream of it; much less should we who are versed in history and philosophy, be moved by such deceptive reasoning.

"Tell me, now, what thy Master intended, when he said that 'neither men nor genii, let them strive Sura xvii. 89.
together never so hard, could produce a book like unto the Coran.' If the contention be that the language surpasseth all other composition in eloquence, our answer is that every nation regardeth its own language the most beautiful, while the Arabs hold every other tongue but their own as barbarous; and similarly the Arabic, held by them as the most beautiful, is regarded by other nations to be barbarous."

"If the claim be that (apart from all other tongues) the Coran is an unparalleled and miraculous model of Arabic (according to the text, *Verily We have sent down the Coran in the Arabic tongue, if perchance ye may comprehend*); then, why do we find in it foreign words, as *namâric* from the Persian, and *mishkât* from the Abyssinian, vocabulary?[2] Here is a defect either in the messenger or the message. If there be in the Arabic language no words to express the ideas, then the medium of communication, and therefore the message itself, is imperfect; if otherwise, the messenger." That not the former, but the latter, was the case, Al Kindy enforces by the congenial argument that there were poets, such as Imrul Cays, and men of eloquence and oratory, without number before Mahomet, whose productions surpassed his, both in conception and language. This was cast in his teeth by the Meccans; for he turns round and calls them 'a contentious race.' And, indeed, Mahomet himself admits as much when he attributes their compositions to magic.[3] The introduction then of foreign expressions into the Coran must be owing to one of two things; either to the poverty of the Arabian vocabulary, while confessedly it is the richest and most copious of all tongues, or to the fact that different persons had a hand in the work; and our Author leaves his Friend on the horns of this dilemma.

Foreign words in the Coran (85-86).

Sura xii. 2; xliii. 2.[1]

Sura xliii. 57.

"If, again, the claim put forth be, that there is in the Coran a supernatural harmony and cadence of language, and beauty of conception; that will be determined by the accuracy of the measures, the purity and fitness of the composition, and the point and charm of thought and imagery. But thy book throughout is broken

Claim of poetical beauty.

[1] See also Sura xiii. 40; xx. 111; xxxix. 28; xli. 2; xlii. 6; and xlvi. 12.

[2] *Namâric*, carpets or cushions; *mishkât*, a lamp; *sandus*, silk; *alastabrac*, satin, brocade; *abârick*, goblets, are also quoted as foreign words imported into the Coran. The argument here may appear singular to us; but to the Arabs, who piqued themselves on the fulness and purity of their language, it would have a force of its own; and it was no doubt of a kind favourably received at Court.

[3] The imputation was often made by the Meccans, as against Mahomet (Sura xxxiv. 2; xliii. 29; xlvi. 6). But here Mahomet apparently is represented as attributing to magic the eloquence of profane writers, which can therefore be no proper test of a revelation.

in its rhythm, confused in its composition, and in its flights of fancy unmeaning."

Matter revealed in the Coran.

Yet once more, if the claim rest on the matter revealed in the Coran, Al Kindy asks what single truth we find there revealed, unknown to the ancients, and which had not already been handled threadbare. In their own day, they were pursuing every branch of knowledge to results unparalleled before; yet what had that to do with such superhuman conditions as were required for miracles like those of Moses or of Christ? The truth, in short, was that the Coran with its manifold defects could only have appeared a miracle of eloquence and learning in the eyes of rude ignorant tribes and barbarous races.

The three false prophets of his time played the same game as Mahomet; and our Author had read passages given out by Moseilama, which would have drawn away the Moslems after him, if only he had had Helpers to support him like those of Mahomet.[1]

Our Apologist here reminds his Friend that the Arabic tongue was the inheritance equally of them both, being derived from their common ancestor Yárob, the great-grandson of Ishmael. Here they stood on the same ground; and in the ability to judge of its beauties and defects, his Friend had no advantage over him. It was, moreover, a vain and deceptive test as addressed to strange nations; for when the Coran was delivered to them, these could not understand it, but were obliged to take the same on trust, and act upon it so far as their ignorance would admit. The Arabs of the desert alone spoke the language in its purity. Such as lived in cities, by intercourse with foreigners, soon lost the simplicity of their tongue, and were incapable of passing any judgment upon it. His Friend might reply that the Coreish were themselves the most eloquent of the Arabs and skilful in the language, and that they were consequently in a position to press the argument; which Al Kindy

[1] I do not know to what utterances of Moseilama our Author can here allude, for the sayings attributed to him by tradition are the veriest rubbish that can well be conceived.

answers by a characteristic declamation on the superiority of his own ancestry. "Thou wilt not deny that when thy Master sought the hand of Muleika, daughter of Nomân Al Kindy, she answered, *What, shall Muleika marry into a race of merchantmen?* Thou knowest well that the Coreish were the traders of Arabia, and the Beni Kinda its Princes. I do not say this vaunting my own descent over thine; but simply to remind thee that the Beni Kinda were the chiefest among the Arabs in eloquence, both oratorical and poetical. Their Kings, foremost in the land, led the armies of Arabia; and so great was their fame that the Persians and Romans were proud to seek their daughters in marriage. At the same time all the world must admit the glory of the Coreish, and especially of the Beni Hâshim; and, indeed, the same applieth to the whole Arab race, whom the Lord hath distinguished by their noble qualities over all the nations upon earth."

Reverting once more to the admission of solecisms into the Coran, it might be urged in defence that the Arabic language was embodied in its poetry; that its vocabulary, drawn from that source, was limited thereby, and that the word for carpets (*namârick*) was unknown. True, our apologist replies; but that arose from the simplicity of the Arab race, who were innocent of the luxuries and refinements of artificial living. In process of time, the language became depraved by foreign words; and in this mongrel tongue people began to make verses, which so aped the ancient poetry of the Peninsula, that it was difficult to distinguish the real from the counterfeit. Now-a-days even learned rhetoricians mistook the spurious for the genuine. The grace and freshness of the tongue, as well as its capacity for carrying on the business of life, had so popularized Arabic, that foreign ideas, and metaphors strange to artless Arab life, were clothed in language claiming to be cast in the ancient mould. And so any one now wrote poetry in the ancient form, and sought thereby courtly favour and advancement. Hence Arabic poetry had become interpolated and corrupted, so that it could not in any way be brought forward, otherwise than as a language changed and debased, in an argument affecting books that relate to the Divine mysteries.[1]

WORLDLY INDUCEMENTS for the propagation of Islam (90-92).

The use in the Coran of terms of luxury and artificial life, introduces a new subject, namely, the material inducements contributing to the propagation of Islam. The Arabs, as every one acquainted with history knew, were a needy and barbarous race, feeding on lizards and such like, with no shelter from the hot blast of summer, nor covering from the cold winds of winter, hungry and naked. What could they know of rivers of wine and milk; rare fruits and viands; couches of silk and satin spread with velvet cushions upon brocaded carpets; ladies, like pearls hiding in their shells; beautiful pages handing round goblets; delicious shade with murmuring rivulets—things appertaining rather to the palaces of the Chosroes.[2] But travellers brought home from Persia the rumour of these marvellous luxuries; and so hearing led to coveting; and coveting, to fighting for the same. His Friend would remember the occasion when the invading Moslem army seized baskets laden with the choice things of Persia; and as they tasted the delicacies thereof, they spake one to another,—*By the Lord! even if there were no Faith to fight for, it were worth our while to fight for this.*[3] And so they fought against an impious nation over whom the Lord gave them the victory; so that they slew them and destroyed their dwellings, for that they had rebelled and shed innocent blood. Even thus doth the Lord visit the sins of stiff-necked peoples, by setting one up against the other.

Al Kindy proceeds to enumerate various classes brought over to Islam, by sordid and unworthy motives. There were first the mongrel boors of the neighbouring Chaldean delta

[1] On this deterioration of language and imitation of ancient poetry, see *Bemerkungen über die Aechtheit der alter Arab. Gedichte*, by Professor Ahlwardt, Greifswald, 1872; also *Beitrage zur Kenntniss der Poesie der alten Araber*, by Theodor Nöldeke, Hannover, 1864; also an Article by myself on *Ancient Arabic Poetry, its Genuineness and Authenticity*, Royal Asiatic Society's Journal, 1879.

[2] All these luxuries are mentioned in the Coran as appertaining to Paradise; see for example Suras xxxvi. 41; liii. 23; lvi. 17.

[3] These words were used by Khâlid in a speech to his army after one of his early victories in Irâc.

(al Sawâd);—"You may address them in Arabic, and they may move their tongue, like a parrot, in reply; but they are mongrel still. Some retain at heart the dregs of their old Jewish and Magian faith; others, blown about by the wind of the day, cannot tell you the distinction between themselves, the brute creation, and their Maker; reared with the beasts of the field they are like them,—"nay more erring and stupid than they." Again, there are the idolatrous races, Magians, and Jews; low people, aspiring by the profession of Islam, to raise themselves to riches and power, and form alliances with the learned and honourable. Then there are hypocritical men of the world, who in this way obtain indulgences in marriage and concubinage, forbidden to them by the Christian faith. There is, moreover, the dissolute class given over wholly to the lusts of the flesh, who take Islam as a ladder to attain their object. Lastly, there are those who by this means obtain an easier livelihood.

Sura vii. 180; xxv. 45.

"Now tell me, hast thou ever seen, my Friend (the Lord be gracious unto thee!) or ever heard, of a single person of sound mind,—any one of learning and experience, acquainted with the Scriptures,—renouncing Christianity otherwise than for some such worldly object to be reached only through thy religion, or for some gratification withheld by the faith of Jesus? Thou wilt find none; for excepting the tempted ones, all continue steadfast in their faith, secure under our most gracious Sovereign, each in the profession of his own religion."

Apostate heretics denounced (93, 94).

Certain classes of apostates and heretics are here described in bitter terms; hypocrites who contemned the Prophet and questioned his claims in secret, while outwardly pluming themselves in his faith. There were heretics who held that the Holy Ghost was divided into three portions, given one to Jesus, another to Moses, and the third to a certain person whose name Al Kindy had a horror even to mention;[1]—Mahomet having no lot or part therein. These were the most

[1] I do not know to what person allusion is here made, and again below at p. 36.

heathenish and detestable of schismatics. Then there were Christian renegades, who used their profession to lord it over innocent and faithful brethren of their old faith,—wolves ravening the lambs, as our Saviour had foretold. The blasphemies of this Satanic brood were beyond description. They boasted that they could produce traditions to prove anything they liked. What would his Friend say of their profanity in pretending that the Lord had sent to Abu Bekr, saying, "O Abu Bekr, I am well pleased with thee; art thou likewise well pleased with me?"[1] It was the old tale,—there was no prophet but his followers fabricated lies about him. Of a similar kind were the mass of contradictory traditions about the Call to prayer, Funeral rites, Prayers, Fasts, Festivals, etc., which it would be wearisome to detail, and his Friend knew it all. The passage is wound up with a scathing denunciation of these hypocritical and blasphemous liars. He had spared the mention of their calumnies against the existing Government, the name of Islam, Prophets, Holy men, etc. But their profanities (like those he had mentioned) were so horrible, the wonder was that they were not destroyed by a thunderbolt, or that the heavens did not fall down and crush them. It was only the mercy and longsuffering of God that spared them and gave space for repentance.

The name of Mahomet written on the Throne of God (94-96).

Al Kindy now addresses himself to the Moslem conceit,—advanced by his Friend in exaltation of Islam,—that before Creation the Almighty had inscribed upon the great Throne the Prophet's name with the Moslem creed, *There is no God but the Lord and Mahomet is the Apostle of God.* He asks, in playful irony, whether this was written up for the benefit of the Angels lest they should forget it,—as if those who sang the praises of their Maker when He said, *Let there be light*, were likely to forget any of His works. Or, was it for the benefit of mankind? If so, how were they

[1] As usual the illustrations go in depreciation of Abu Bekr, as was the fashion of the Alyites at Al Mâmûn's Court. A few reigns later, no one would have dared to repeat traditions affecting the character of the first three Caliphs.

to see it, while here on earth? and in the Day of Judgment, the truth would be too clearly set before the eyes of all, to need any adventitious help. He scouts the notion as unworthy of his Friend; and adds that he never heard of any of the companions of his Friend who shared his views, or indeed of any wise and intelligent Moslem who did not reject the tale. The idea was a preposterous and ignoble fancy borrowed from the corporeal conception of the Jews that God was seated on a material throne.

Argument from the seed of Abraham being "preferred above all mankind" (96, 97).

"It is customary for your preachers (he proceeds) to open an address by the following invocation:—*O Lord, bless Mahomet and the posterity of Mahomet, even as Thou hast blessed Abraham and the posterity of Abraham;* and having so said, they think that they have exhausted all that can possibly be invoked in the way of blessing. Now consider the horrid impiety of connecting thus a person (Mahomet) whose name ye imagine to be written with that of the Most High on the Throne of Light and on whose behalf alone Adam and the world were created,—connecting with the name of such an one, the seed of Abraham including a person whom thou knowest, but whose name I should tremble to write in this place.[1] But indeed the superiority of the Israelites over all other nations is reiterated in various passages of the Coran itself, as,—'O children of Israel, remember the Favour wherewith I have favoured you, and preferred you above all mankind,'—preferred therefore above thee, and above thy Master, upon whom in the aforesaid prayer thou invoked the blessing of Abraham." This was mentioned as a mere *argumentum ad hominem*, and not by any means as conveying his own sentiments. For he had throughout carefully avoided reference to race or superior descent,—seeing that all mankind were of one blood, children of a common parent,—the only difference between man and man being in mind and virtue. And in saying even so much as he had, he deprecates the

Sura ii. 47, 123.

[1] Again, I do not know to what descendant of Abraham reference is here intended,—so detestable that Al Kindy will not even mention his name.

vulgar aspersion which the ignorant and spiteful might cast upon him, as if he had sought to slight the Royal house, the Prophet's family, or any of his race.

Al Kindy now comes to the various Moslem ceremonies he had been recommended to adopt. Of Prayer and Fasting, it sufficed to say that his Friend had confessed himself acquainted with those duties as performed in a far diviner way under the Christian dispensation. In respect of ceremonial washings, he quotes our Saviour's words as teaching the vanity of outward cleansing while there was a foul sepulchre within. "What sense is there in the washing of your hands and feet and your standing up to prayer while your hearts are set upon bloodshed and rapine and the ravishing of women? Hath not our Lord the Christ given us a better lesson,—Cleanse first that which is within, that the outside may be clean also?" In respect of Circumcision, he reminds his Friend, that he himself, along with those of his persuasion, held that Mahomet was not circumcised. If the precedent of Jesus were urged, he answers that he was circumcised simply to fulfil the Law;—which law, in its Sacrifices, Sabbaths, Passover, etc., ("statutes that were not good") having been fulfilled by Christ, had disappeared in place of ordinances far superior, because entirely spiritual. St. Paul teaches us that circumcision is nothing; and, if trusted in, worse than nothing. In short, both washing and circumcision were things indifferent; if practised by Christians it was simply by way of habit and ancestral custom, and not of obligation.[1]

Ordinances of Islam (96-98).

Matt. v. 17. Ezek. xx. 25.

1 Cor. vii. 19; Gal. v. 2.

The prohibition of swine's flesh is combated on the ground that God made all things "very good," and that nothing in nature was unholy or forbidden;—excepting only blood, and that which

Gen. i. 31.

Prohibition of swine's flesh (100-102).

1 There are several passages which must be omitted here. *Page* 98, last eight lines. The reason assigned for circumcision is both childish and indelicate. *Page* 100, first five lines may be true, but the mode of expression is gross and offensive. *Page* 102, lower half (and by consequence first seven lines of page 103), relating to Hagar, and a practice current among the Arabs (*Life of Mahomet*, 1st edition, vol. ii. p. 108, note), is at once silly and grossly improper. It is strange that a man of refinement should have admitted such a passage into his book. But it is the habit of the Arabs (see *Life of Mahomet*, p. 600), and the laxity of Islam has not improved it.

dieth of itself, and things offered to idols, for these were unlawful by command of the Lord. The reason assigned for the Mosaic prohibition is curious. The Egyptians worshipped kine, goats, etc., as their gods;[1] while, on the contrary, they held swine, horses, camels, etc., to be unclean, and offered them in sacrifice to their gods. To disabuse the Israelites of such idolatrous notions, the sacred animals were sacrificed to the True God, and their flesh allowed to be eaten; while the other animals deemed unclean by the Egyptians were forbidden to be either sacrificed or eaten. As to pork, there was no more reason why it should be prohibited than the flesh of the camel, ass, or horse, allowed by Mahomet. It was a matter indifferent, in which each was free to follow his taste and fancy. The prohibition is moreover set down to the pernicious teaching of Abdallah ibn Sallam, the Jew, who had depraved the faith; and for this Mahomet himself was nowise responsible.

PILGRIMAGE and rites of Mecca (103-108).

The invitation to observe the Pilgrimage and Meccan rites, is derided by Al Kindy, as if his Friend took him for a child or a fool. "Knowest thou not that the same is the practice of the Sun-worshippers and Brahmas in India at the present day? They make the circuit of their idol Temples, with just these ceremonies, shaved and naked (or with the dress they call *ihrâm*). The only difference is that ye perform it once in the year at a moveable season, while they do it twice at certain solar conjunctions, one in the Spring when the heat begins, the other in Autumn when the cold sets in.[2] Such is the origin of these idolatrous customs. Thou well knowest that the Arabs practised them from the foundation of the Káaba; and thy Master continued the same, with only this alteration, that on account of the distance and labour of travel, he limited the Pilgrimage to one period of the year, and abolished what was indecent

[1] In proof he adduces Exod. viii. 26; and also the worship of the golden calf, a relic of Egypt.

[2] Our familiar Indian terms *Rubbee* and *Khurreef* are given for the Spring and Autumn festivals.

in the pilgrim dress.[1] Thus, that which ye perform in nothing differs from the idolatrous ceremonies of the Sun-worshippers and Idolators of India. There is a saying attributed to Omar as he stood by the Black Stone and the Station (of Abraham);[2] 'By the Lord! I know that neither of these Stones can benefit, nor hurt; but I have seen the Prophet kiss them both, and therefore I do the same.' Now whether they spake false or true in attributing this utterance to Omar, they certainly spake what is true as regardeth the Stones themselves." Shaving the head, making bare the body, running the prescribed circuits, and casting the small Stones at Minâ, senseless and unmeaning rites, were defended by some as acts of service to the Deity; but the worship of God should be conducted, not by unfit and foolish practices, but by observances consonant with reason, pleasing to the Almighty, and edifying to His servants. If otherwise, then why abandon the objectionable customs of the Magians, who thought it lawful to take to wife their own mothers, sisters, and daughters, and other such like abominations. "But what could be more vile (he seizes the opportunity of adding) than your own ordinance for legalizing re-marriage after the thrice repeated divorce; for by it, a chaste lady, tender and delicate, the mother of virtuous daughters, herself it may be noble-born and held in honour by her kinsfolk,—this pattern of virtue and refinement must submit her person to the lewd embrace of a hired gallant, before she can be restored to her husband,—an abominable law, more odious even than the wicked customs of the Magians. And yet thou invitest me to accept a vile ordinance like this,—an ordinance against which the very beasts of the field, if ye gave them speech, would cry out for shame![3] God forbid that

[1] Our Author is at fault here; for the only change made by Mahomet in the season of pilgrimage was to abolish the intercalary month, so that the pilgrimage shifts with the lunar, instead of being stationary, according to the luni-solar year. *Life of Mahomet*, p. 486.

[2] The *Macâm*. See *Life of Mahomet*, p. 423 (also 1st edition, vol. ii. p. 38).

[3] Al Kindy's words are strong, but not too strong, here. See *Life of Mahomet*, page 350.

I should so do violence to my reason and my nature; the Lord save me from being amongst the transgressors!

"Thou invitest me to visit the Holy places, 'those blessed and marvellous spots,' as thou callest them. 'Marvellous,' in truth, my Friend, must those places be where rites are witnessed so repugnant to common sense. But as for being 'blessed,' I wish to know what blessing hath ever flowed from visiting them. The sick, the maimed, the leper the possessed of the devil,—hath any one of them ever returned whole from thence? Such blessings are known only to the Christian faith. The Lord's are open to the cry wheresoever it ariseth from an earnest heart; and Christ hath promised that where any two shall agree in prayer as touching anything, it shall be granted." Al Kindy then dilates, with much apparent complacency, on the cures which, at the intercession of Monks, Priests, and Holy men of God, were wrought in churches, monasteries, and other sacred places, where men were wont to call on the name of the Lord. Through such intercession, blessings descended on the humble and the pious; and even the wicked, if they returned, would be graciously received, as our Author shows in the words of the parable of the Prodigal Son.[1]

"Distinguish now, my Friend, between thy Faith and mine, and let not misguided zeal mislead thee, for that is naught but Satan's guile, according to the text: 'Satan verily is the enemy of mankind.' Seest thou not (the Lord have mercy on thee!) that thou art calling me from an unspeakable priceless blessing, coveted by the Angels, and longed for by Prophets and Kings, and Holy men of old, to that which my soul loatheth, and which is utterly repugnant to my reason. Were I to consent, I trow not that I should be among the faithful."

Sura xii. 6; xvii. 53; xx. 30.

The Saracenic crusade (108-121).

"And then, thou callest on me 'to enter on *The way of the Lord*,' that is to wage war against other religions, to smite with the sword, and

[1] In this section, which I have more than usually abbreviated, quotations are given from Ps. xxxiv. and cxlv.; Matt. xviii. 19; x. 8; and Luke xv.

make slaves of mankind, until they confess 'that there is no God but the Lord, and that Mahomet is his Servant and Apostle;' or, if they refuse, 'until they pay tribute with their hands and are humbled.' Dost thou indeed desire (may the Lord enlighten thee!) that I should work the works of Satan, the bereft of mercy, who first himself beguiled mankind, and then, by filling them with hate and bitterness, hath made them his tools, to carry out thereby his devilish ends of murder, rape, and rapine.

"Now tell me how thou wilt reconcile the two sets of passages that follow (for they are confessedly discordant) out of the book thou holdest to be divine? CONTRADICTORY PASSAGES. 'Let there be a people amongst you who invite to that which is just, enjoin the right and forbid the evil; these shall be blessed.' Sura iii. 104. Again, 'The direction of them appertaineth not unto thee; but rather, the Lord directeth whom he pleaseth.' Sura ii. 273. And more forcibly still: 'Had the Lord so pleased, verily all that are on the earth would have believed, every one; Wilt thou, then, compel men to become believers, seeing that no soul can believe but by command (or permission) of God?' Sura x. 98. Seest thou not how these commands are inconsistent with force? Hear yet again: 'SAY, O men, the truth hath verily now come unto you from your Lord; he, therefore, that is rightly directed, is directed for the benefit of his own soul; and he that erreth, erreth only against the same; I am no Guardian over you. Do thou (O Mahomet) follow that which is revealed unto thee. Be patient until the Lord decide; for he is the best of all Deciders.' Sura x. 107. Similarly, in another text: 'If thy Lord had pleased, he had made all men of one faith; but they shall not cease to differ among themselves, excepting those upon whom thy Lord hath mercy; and unto this hath he created them.' Sura xi. 119. Again, thy Master reiterates emphatically, that he *Was sent with Mercy to the human race.*[1] 'Mercy,'

[1] The words are not quoted literally; but the expression occurs in more than one passage, as Sura xxi. 107; xxviii. 47.

in slaying, plundering, and enslaving! The Jews accuse thy book of contradicting itself. I will use no such opprobrious expression towards the book; but what I say is that thou, my Friend, contradictest thyself. Thou art never weary of crying up thy faith as divine; and anon thou turnest clean round, and sayest just the opposite; for what after all, are these doings,—killing and shedding of blood, rapine and robbery, and making slaves of men and women,—what are they, but the works of the Devil?

"If the precedent of Moses and Joshua be urged, I demand miracles such as they wrought to justify the commission. Moreover, they fought against idolators; but here, the horrors of war, bloodshed, rapine, and slavery are hurled against the innocent, nay, against the people of God,—those who observe His ordinances, devote soul and body to His service, believe in His Messiah, worship Him and are guided into the right way,—those whose Leaders are blessed and renowned both in this world and the next.

"Still further, thou art not content with this, but insistest on calling it 'The Way of the Lord.' God forbid that that should be His way, or that His children should commit such crimes; for He loveth not the transgressors. And then thou hast it revealed, in direct contradiction thereof,

Sura ii. 25. —'Let there be no constraint in religion.'

Sura iii. 20. And, 'Say unto those who have received the 'Scriptures, and to the Gentiles,—Do ye embrace Islam? 'Now, if they embrace it, they are surely guided aright; 'but, if they turn their backs, verily unto thee (O Prophet) 'belongeth delivery of the message only, for God observeth

Sura ii. 254. 'His servants.' And again, 'If the Lord had 'so willed, those who came after them (*i.e.* after the Apostles 'and Jesus) would not have contended among themselves, 'after manifest signs had been shown unto them. But 'they fell to variance. Some believed, and some believed 'not. And if God had so pleased, they had not so contended. 'But the Lord doeth as it so pleaseth Him.' And yet again, addressing the Unbelievers (Kâfirs), thy Master is bidden to say, 'Ye have your religion, and I have mine.' And finally, 'Contend not with the People of the Book,[1] but in the way that is most mild and gracious.' And then thou stirrest up thy people to attack mankind with the sword, to plunder them, and lead them away captive, that they may be forced to embrace the faith by violence and against their will. Which of the two directions am I to follow, the first or the last?

Sura cix.

Sura xxix. 46.

"Thou wilt say, then, that one of the two sets of texts is cancelled by the other. But which cancelleth, and which is cancelled, thou canst not show. Thou hast confessedly neither proof nor certain knowledge in this matter; and it may be that thou mistakest the one for the other. How are we to discriminate the true from the false, for the two sets of passages both being in thy Book, are directly opposed the one to the other; and there is this risk that the one which thou regardest as true, and on which thou art bound to act, may be the one that is false and therefore to be abandoned; so that really each counteracteth the other, and neither can be the command of the Lord.

One set of passages cancelled by the other.

"And, now, say,—Hath it ever reached thine ears, or hast thou ever read in any book, sacred or profane, of a preacher, other than thy Master, imposing his creed by force, or summoning men to believe, against their conscience, by sword and threat, rapine and slavery? Even the abhorred Magians claim that inspiration descended on Zerdasht, at the hill Sailân, and that Kashtasaf and his people believed on seeing the miracle of the dead horse brought to life again, and that the ten thousand volumes of the Zenda-vesta were revealed in every human tongue (which yet if ye ask the meaning thereof no one knoweth). After the same manner is the miracle of the Phœnix wrought by Bood in India, from the bowels of which a damsel issued, prophesying, and testifying that Bood was a divine image, and his doctrine true. These are but examples.

[1] That is, Jews and Christians.

And so, my Friend, thou wilt find in history mention of no teacher, true or false, who did not advance some kind of proof, to be weighed in the scales of right and wrong, excepting only thy Master; for he used no other argument that I can see, but the sword. Nor wilt thou hear of any other but he, standing up and saying,—*Whoever doth not accept me as a Prophet and the Apostle of God, the same shall be slain, his goods seized, and his women and children carried off captive*;—and all this without a tittle of evidence!

"As for the ministry of our blessed Saviour, it is too sacred and excellent to be brought into comparison here. Thou knowest it all. Now say, my Friend, doth it become a man of thine intelligence and culture to ask one like me, who have devoted my life to the study of men and things, to embrace a faith like this,—I who read the words of the Saviour,—my garment and my righteousness,—night and day: hearken to His gracious voice:—'Be tender unto all mankind, and merciful; that ye may be like unto your Father in Heaven, for He causeth his sun to shine on the good and on the bad, and sendeth down his rain upon the righteous and upon the wicked.' How should I, with these words ringing in my ears,—I who have been nurtured in this blessed faith of Grace and Mercy,—so that it hath become part of my flesh, my bones, my blood, my very life,—God forbid that I should harden my heart and become rebellious, changed into the image of Iblîs, the Enemy and Murderer; and should smite with the sword, and slay children of mine own species, the seed of Adam formed by the hand of the Almighty, and in the likeness of the Most High;—He that saith, 'I desire not the death of the sinner, who is to-day in his sins, and on the morrow, if he repent, I will receive him as a tender Father doth.'" There follows a glowing description of the glory and honour bestowed on humanity by the Son of God having taken our nature, and as such worshipped by angels and endowed with all power in heaven and earth,—our Brother, seated at the right hand of the Majesty on high, to come hereafter as the Judge of men, angels, and devils. "Wilt thou, my Friend, that I, rejecting His grace and favour, should destroy and enslave mine own species, ennobled thus and allied with the Divine nature? God forbid! I flee to the Lord for refuge, from His wrath and indignation!"

Should his Friend urge, as an analogy, that God sends death, famine, and such like calamities on mankind, our Apologist would reply (not with the childish answer his Friend once made, in a former discussion "on the soul," that *God made it so,*) as follows. "The Lord sendeth death and calamities upon His servants not because he hateth and seeketh to injure them, for then why should He ever have created mankind, and why seek (as we know He doth) to fulfil them with His grace and mercy and take them from this transitory and imperfect life, to the blessed life above? Rather, these trials and calamities are meant as a probation to prepare for the reward hereafter;—even as a skilful and gracious physician, seeking to recover the sick, giveth bitter medicine and nauseous draughts, now starveth the appetite, and now even burneth with the cautery, or cutteth off a limb with the sharp knife. No one would say that he doeth this from hate or emnity, but to recover his patient from pain and disease, to the blessings of health. But you will say, *God might have made man happy without these trials.* Of course, He might; and even so, He might not have created this earth at all, but have placed man from the first, without trial or trouble, and without any claim of merit, in Paradise. But in His sovereign wisdom, he hath made the world, and this life a pilgrimage, and us as 'Sons of the road' resting for the night as it were in a Khân, that He might, after proving us for a while with trial and hunger, translate us to our reward in the Home above of endless peace and happiness.

"Now if this thy Master, whom thou invitest me to follow, slew, enslaved, scourged, and expatriated men, with the view of raising them to a better state,—by my life! surely he would rather have been patient in admonition, and kind, and gracious,—following therein the example of the High and Holy One. But he did not thus, neither concerned

himself for this end. His aim was the aggrandizement of himself and his fellows, and the establishment of his kingdom
Sura ix. 30. according to his own words,—*Until they pay tribute with their hand and are humbled.* Seest thou not, my clear-sighted Friend, that his desire was not to bring them from infidelity to faith, nor any regard for their well-being and happiness, but like other conquerors, to extend his empire. And yet in the book thou holdest divine, he purporteth to have been commanded thus; 'Say to the people of the Book and to the Gentiles, *Do ye accept Islam?* . . . and if they turn their backs, verily thy duty is only to deliver the message.' Dost thou not perceive that he was commanded to preach with his lips, and forbidden to strike with the sword? Now the Lord enlighten thee, my Friend, and enable thee to escape from the horns of this dilemma!

Moslem Martyrs contrasted with Christian (117-121).

"I marvel much that ye call those Martyrs that fall in war. Thou hast read, no doubt, in history of the followers of Christ put to death in the persecutions of the Kings of Persia and elsewhere. Are these more worthy to be called Martyrs, or thy fellows that fall fighting for the world and the power thereof?" Then follows a description of various barbarities and kinds of death inflicted on the Christian confessors. The more they were slain, the more rapidly spread the faith; in place of one, sprung up a hundred. On a certain occasion, when a great multitude had been put to death, one said to the king, *The number of them increaseth, instead of (as thou thinkest) diminishing.* "How can that be?" exclaimed the king. "Yesterday," replied the Courtier, "thou didst put such and such a one to death, and immediately there were converted just double that number; and the people say that a man appeared to the confessors from heaven, strengthening them at the last moment." The king finding this to be true, was thereupon himself converted, and the persecution stayed. These men thought not their lives dear unto them. Some were transfixed while yet alive; of others, the limbs were cut off one after another. Some were cast to the wild beasts, and others burned in the fire. Such continued long to be the fate of the Christian confessors: no parallel is to be found to it in any other religion: and all was endured with constancy, and even with joy. The story is related of one who smiled in the midst of great suffering:—"Was it cold water," they asked, "that was brought to thee?" "No," answered the Martyr; "but a youth stood by me and anointed my wounds; and that made me smile; for the pain forthwith departed, and seemed as if it entered into my tormentors instead." But this Angel, you may say, could equally well have stayed the hand of the persecutors, and that might have turned to their conversion? To this Al Kindy answers, True, for if God had so willed He might have forced all men into the faith; but then the glory of humanity, which lies in Free-will, would have gone, and with it the merit of obedience based on evidence without miracles. For miracles were needful only to those of the early ages, in order to perfect their faith. But these interpositions are now withdrawn, to make it manifest that obedience is to be grounded on free and intelligent conviction. And if men having this evidence refuse the truth, except they see miracles, the Lord leaveth them in their error.

With all this, however, our Apologist holds that the virtue of working miracles, though latent, still survives in the Christian Church; and of all religions in it alone. He had seen with his own eyes, as well as heard on sufficient evidence, of cures wrought by the clergy and monks in their holy places, tombs, and churches dedicated to the Christian martyrs, and also in virtue of their bones and relics. It was so in every land of the East and West, excepting only the land of Mahomet, for in Arabia there never had been any of this class, saving only Sergius and Bahîra.[1]

"Now looking with an impartial eye, tell me seriously, my Friend, which of these two hath the best claim to be called a Martyr 'slain in the ways of the Lord'; he

[1] Our Author need not have forgotten the Christians of Najrân with their Bishop Coss, and the martyrs of the Fiery Pits. See *Life of Mahomet*, pp. v, and 81, and Sura lxxxv.

who surrendereth his life rather than renounce his faith,—who when it is said, Fall down and worship the sun and moon, or the idols of silver and gold work of men's hands, instead of the True God,—refuseth, choosing rather to give up life, abandon wealth, and forego even wife and family; —or he that goeth forth, ravaging and laying waste, plundering and spoiling, slaying the men, carrying off their children into captivity, and ravishing their wives and maidens in his unlawful embrace; and then shall call it *Jehâd in the ways of the Lord*, and shall say of him that slayeth or is slain that 'he hath inherited Paradise.' Judge aright, my Friend, in this matter. If a robber plundering a house, should fall into a well, or the wall fall down upon him, or the owner rush out and strike him, so that he die; would blood-money at all be claimable for such a one? I trow that no Cadhee would so decide. How then shall paradise be to him who falleth upon a people unawares, secure and at peace in their homes,—he knowing not them, nor they him; plundering, enslaving, and ravishing? And, not content therewith, instead of humbling thyself before the Lord and seeking pardon for the crime,—thou sayest of such a one, whether he slay or be slain, that 'he hath earned Paradise,' and thou namest him 'a Martyr in the ways of the Lord'! If such be thy judgment, it is naught but the judgment of Satan, the Enemy of Adam and his race from of old. But well I know that thy reason and justice both forbid it."

He pauses to apologize for the warmth of his language. Sparks will fly from the flint when it is struck by steel. It was his friend himself who had enlarged the sphere of the discussion; and there had been much need for the stipulated forbearance on either side. Moreover, his argument was intended not merely for his friend, but for all who should read his book.

Temporal inducements offered by Islam (121-123).

Of the temporal enjoyments held out as a motive for his conversion, he says that these flit past like a dream of the night, or the lightning which, dazzling the eye of the bystander for a moment, leaves him in deeper darkness. Such was not the chief end of a rational and immortal being.

Holy men of God sought rather to be freed from these allurements. The Coran tells us that the Almighty "created Men and Genii only that they might serve Him." That was the true end of man: and now his Friend turned round and tried inconsistently to snare him with this bait,—*Marry such women as are pleasing to thee, two, three, or four; and slave-girls without stint;*[1] eat, drink, and enjoy life like the beasts that have no restraint either of reason or revelation. As for the change of wives, and especially the "thrice repeated divorce," he had already dwelt upon it,—the latter being an abomination, denounced by the prophet Jeremiah, and by all other creeds and nations; and he would not defile his book by dwelling further on the revolting subject.

Sura li. 56.

Jeremiah iii. 1 Deut. xxiv. 4.

Thanks given for guarantee of security (123).

Coming now near to the close of his argument against Islam, our Author thankfully acknowledges the guarantee of immunity in the free treatment of their discussion. Our Saviour, indeed, bade us not to fear him who hath power over the body only, but to fear the Creator of both soul and body. Nevertheless Al Kindy had gained additional freedom and assurance from the just and impartial rule of the Commander of the Faithful, who always protected the weak like himself, and under the shadow of whose benign and powerful sceptre, the Christian community reposed in comfort and security. And he besought the Lord, who answered the prayers of His faithful servants, to grant every worldly blessing both to his august Person and to his Family.

Our Apologist will not be dazzled by the distinctions held out (123, 124).

Referring, once more, to his Friend's invitation to share with him the honours and dignities of the realm and the rank proper to his distinguished birth, our Apologist says that the Lord truly had bestowed upon the kindred of his Friend the Caliphate, with all its honours and distinctions; and long might it remain safe and intact

[1] Page 20.

in the Abbasside line of the Prophet's house. But, as for the glory that remaineth, there was none but that which arose from a holy life. The Prophet himself, addressing his people, said, "O ye seed of Abd Menâf, birth and dignity shall profit nought either for me or for you: verily, with the Lord, the best of you is the holiest." And truly, Holy men of God have mostly had little to boast of in race or blood or worldly greatness. Their piety was their nobility; the world to come, their inheritance. Our Apologist had no desire to parade his ancestry, descended though he was from the Kings of the Beni Kinda, whose authority was once acknowledged over all Arabia; for as the apostle Paul had said, *He that glorieth, let him glory in the Lord.* Beyond that glory he had no ambition. His boast was in the faith of Christ, whom to know was Life eternal.

Promise of Mahomet's intercession (124, 125).

The Hâshimite had spoken of the need of the Prophet's advocacy in the Day of Judgment, when he would cry aloud, "These are my kin; these are my people!" and his intercession would prevail.[1] "My dearest Friend," answers Al Kindy, "are thine eyes asleep, or dreaming, that thou utterest such senilities? There is no shadow of doubt but that our Lord Jesus Christ,—the same as is borne testimony to in thine own book,—in that day will be sole Judge, rendering by the strictest rule of right, to every man according to his deeds, be they good or evil. Righteousness alone will then avail." Let not his Friend be beguiled by the lying vanities of the world. The march was swift; death was near; the day at hand, when we must all stand before the Judgment-seat, and then repentance, excuse, and supplication would be all too late. And so he ends an earnest personal appeal, of which I have contented myself with giving the mere outline.

Islam an easy religion (125, 126).

"Thou invitest me (he continues), to the *Easy way of faith and practice.* Alas, alas! and our Saviour telleth us in the Gospel, When ye have done all that ye are commanded, say, *We are unprofitable ser-*

[1] Page 19.

vants; we have done that which was commanded us, and where is our merit? The same Lord Jesus saith, 'How straight is the road which leadeth unto life, and how few they that walk therein! how wide the gate that leadeth to destruction, and many there be who go in thereat!' Different this, my Friend, from the facilities of thy wide and easy gate, and thine advice to me to enjoy the pleasures offered by thy faith in wives and damsels!" Then he prays that God would guide his Friend from such deceits and errors into the right way, and from the darkness in which he was shrouded into the marvellous light of the Gospel. Such prayers (he adds) are constantly put up by the Christian Church for all sorts and conditions of men,—that sinners might be converted, and the faithful built up. "May the Lord fulfil the same for thee and for all our brethren!"

The Trinity defended from his adversary's abuse (126, 127).

He now proceeds to answer the double objection,—that to acknowledge the Trinity, and to worship the Cross, are both of them "blasphemy and error." The first our Author (having disposed of it before) treats here but briefly. Moslems called the doctrine of the Trinity *takhlît* (confusion of essence), but so in truth they call everything which they do not comprehend, according to the proverb, *Man is an enemy to whatever he doth not understand,*—"a principle from which the Lord defend us!" That which they call *takhlît* was an ineffable mystery before the Creation; and thereafter, the angels and cherubim, prophets and holy men of God, desired to look into the little that was revealed of it by distant adumbration; until the Son himself came and unfolded the same;—as when He said,—"Go and call all nations to the true and perfect knowledge, that which is in the name of the Father, and of the Son, and of the Holy Ghost." The Apostles received this commission from His sacred lips, and handed it down to us, the whole company of believers, accompanied by signs and wonders; and we stand firmly upon the same, and will, by the grace of God, do so to the end of time.

The adoration of the Cross is dwelt upon at greater length, but may be disposed of briefly here. It was not the Cross they worshipped, but the power that rested in it as a symbol, the strength derived therefrom, and the redemption wrought out upon the same. "We reverence it, as we reverence symbols of royalty; even as the Israelites reverenced the Ark, not the wooden material, but the presence which it signified;[1] and so we follow the example of prophets and holy men, when we do homage to the Cross." Here he takes the opportunity of bringing home to his friend the inconsistency between his practice and profession, for it seems that he had been in the habit, when in sudden peril, of invoking the Cross, or using the sign, as a safeguard. Repeated occasions are quoted when this had happened to his friend;—once on falling from his beast; again when he fled from some danger; and yet again when on a journey to Omar al Karakh, a lion started up before them as they neared Sabât al Medâin.[2] He refers also to an assembly in which his Friend seems to have recognized and avowed the practice. "And now," says Al Kindy, "thou writest as if it were a superstition which bringeth no good, but hurt. I should like to know what hath changed thy mind; and what hurt the appeal to the Cross hath ever caused thee?"

Adoration of the Cross (127-129).

Before passing on to the evidences of Christianity, Al Kindy founds a quaint but affectionate remonstrance on his friend's daily use of the Fâteha. "Thine earnest appeal (he says) deserveth my gratitude as a friendly act; and now if I reverse the appeal to thee, I shall deserve thy thanks with an infinitely deeper meaning. Nay, what need have I to speak, when thou thyself, five times in the day, repeatest in thy prayer,—*Guide us into the straight path, the path of those Thou art gracious unto, not of those with whom Thou art wroth, nor of them*

The *Fâteha*; or daily prayer not to be among those who go away (130-132).

Sura i.

[1] Here he quotes Numbers x. 35; when the Ark was set forward, Moses said, "Rise up, Lord, and let thine enemies be scattered," etc.

[2] A station in Mesopotamia, near Medâin (Ctesiphon).

that go astray. Now, if thou art already rightly guided, what need hast thou to beg with prostration and importunity, in every prayer of thine, to be guided aright? There would thus be no reason in the prayer. If, then, thou art not yet rightly guided, inform me, my Friend (the Lord bless thee!) who those people are on whom God is gracious, and into whose way thou art ever praying, night and day, to be guided. And yet thou claimest to be 'the best people that have been raised up,' and thy faith the most approved of God for thee. Which religion, then, is meant?" Hereupon he enumerates the various religions of the world; the Magians and Jews, both of whom he condemns with characteristic warmth; the idolators of Arabia, Atheists, Brahmas, etc. "And, now, as thou canst not but agree with me in rejecting each and all of these, there remaineth only as 'the faith of those on whom the Lord is gracious,' the Christian faith: that truly is the 'Straight path' which leadeth to the knowledge of God, and his Word, and Spirit, and all the ordinances thereof are spiritual and perfect. I ask thee to accept it, for indeed thou art well acquainted with the same, and canst not gainsay me in thus praising it. To us this gracious Gospel hath been given; thine own Master beareth testimony to it in his book; and all religions bow down before it. Give heed, my Friend, to what I have here put before thee; study it as one that seeketh to have his soul directed aright, not as one that seeketh to beguile the same. Each soul is responsible for the road it taketh. If the truth be truth, then follow the same; it behoveth thee not to stifle conviction. The Lord guide thee aright, and direct thy feet into 'the straight path,' by his power and grace!"

Sura iii. 110.

The remainder of the book is devoted by Al Kindy to the evidences of Christianity and a brief account of the life and teaching of our Saviour. His friend had begged for this;[1] and Al Kindy

An account of THE CHRISTIAN FAITH (132-164).

[1] Page 29.

compliments him as specially qualified, both by natural gifts and by knowledge of the subject, to grasp the argument. He first offers up a prayer that the Holy Spirit's light and guidance might be shed upon his Friend, and all his readers; and then proceeds with his subject.

Old Testament prophecies (133-138).

Eight pages are devoted to the prophecies of the Old Testament, from all parts of which quotations are freely taken. It is unnecessary to say more than that neither in the passages selected, nor in the manner of applying them, does the Apology materially differ from similar treatises in the present day. The section closes with a powerful defence of the Jewish Scriptures against the charge of interpolation and corruption. First we have their common use from the earliest times by Christians as well as Jews, notwithstanding that these are irreconcileably opposed on every other point. Then the Scriptures are attested by the Coran itself:—"If thou art in doubt as to what We have revealed unto thee, then ask those who read the Book (revealed) from before thee,—that verily the truth hath come unto thee from thy Lord, and be not thou among them that doubt." And still more explicitly:—"They to whom we have given the Book read it according to its true reading. These are they that believe therein; and whosoever believeth not therein, they shall be lost." "Our 'reading' is here asserted to be the right one, and thy Master directeth that we (that is the Christians) are to be asked concerning the same, and that what we declare in respect of it must be accepted. How then canst thou accuse us of corruption, or of 'changing the text from its place?' That would be to contradict thyself, and go back from the rule of fair interpretation which we agreed to for the conduct of this argument." He points out further the utter impossibility of collusion. How could nations of different religion, and various sects scattered over every land, agree to falsify their Scriptures? It were an unheard-of thing. Finally, he contrasts the Christian Scriptures with the Moslem, dwelling

Jewish Scriptures uncorrupted (138-140).

Sura x. 93.

Sura ii. 122.

briefly on his former arguments as to the heterogeneous character of the materials and composition of the Coran, and the compulsory enforcement of its acceptance, without miracle or proof, at the point of the sword. "Judge fairly, my Friend; for verily the Lord hath appointed reason and the balance of justice to be the test in this matter; and thou, if thou inquirest sincerely, wilt surely, by the blessing of God, attain unto the Truth."

The Annunciation and Birth of Christ (140-144).

Sura iii. 35, et seq. (42-49).

He then proceeds to the life of our Saviour and the fulfilment of the prophecies that went before. After an account of the Annunciation as given in the Gospels,[1] he quotes at length the corresponding passage from the Coran,[2] and adds:—"This is the story as told by thy Master himself, in attestation of the Gospel history. Now say, my Friend (and the Lord direct thee!) whether thou hast ever heard, or read in books, of any one who was ushered into the world with a blessed annunciation such as I have related to thee from the Gospel, and also from thine own Scripture." There follows Mary's visit to Elizabeth, and the vision of Zecharias (in respect of which the Coran is again quoted as showing that it was the office of John the Baptist to bear witness "to the Word of God"[3]), the Adoration of the Magians, and the Angels' Song to the shepherds.

Sura iii. 39.

Ministry of Christ (145, 146).

He passes on briefly to the Ministry of Christ; his baptism, the testimony of his being the Lamb of God, the Temptation, and Miracles. He dwells on the meekness, humility and kindness of Jesus; and lays stress on his poverty and the absence of any worldly object save only to bring salvation to mankind.

[1] Curiously enough he quotes the Salutation thus:—"The blessing of *our Lord* be with thee:" not *my Lord*, but *ours*; i.e. of angels and men, implying that he is "the Lord of heaven and earth," etc. I do not find this reading anywhere.

[2] "And when the Angels said, O, Mary, verily God hath chosen thee, and sanctified thee, and exalted thee above all the women of the world. O Mary, be devout towards thy Lord, and worship, and bow down with those who bow down . . . O Mary, the Lord giveth thee good tidings of the Word proceeding from himself, called Jesus the Christ, the Son of Mary," etc.

[3] In quoting this passage (مصدقاً بكلمةٍ من الله وسيداً) he applies "lord" (*Syed*) to Jesus, whereas by the construction it must refer to *John*.

A full outline follows of our Saviour's teaching drawn
Teaching of our Saviour (146-155). from the Sermon on the Mount; and a page is devoted to justify the doctrine of the Fatherhood of God. The brotherhood and unity of mankind as flowing therefrom are contrasted with the
Sura lxiv. 15. teaching of the Coran;[1] and the claim of the Almighty to be regarded as a wise and tender Parent is illustrated from Hebrews xii. 6. He dwells upon the
Sura ii. 87, 254, and iii. 48. miracles of Jesus, and shows that they were acknowledged in the Coran. In contrast with the wonderful works done by the Jewish prophets, Jesus performed these by His own inherent power, and never
Jerem. vii. 16. failed as Moses did at the waters of Meriba, or Jeremiah whom the Lord refused to hear.

For his Apostles the Lord chose simple and unlearned
Apostles and disciples sent forth by Christ (155-159). persons, poor fishermen and despised tax gatherers. Through these He overturned all the wisdom and philosophy, the nobility and kingly power that opposed the faith on every hand. The instructions with which the Apostles and the Seventy disciples were sent forth are given in considerable detail, and are summed up with great force and eloquence, in implied contrast with the interested aims, and worldly agencies, of the first propagators of Islam.

The death, resurrection, and ascension of Jesus are
Death and Ascension of Jesus (160). recounted in a very few lines. "Let me add (says our Author) "the testimony of the Coran,—'When God said, O Jesus, verily I 'will cause thee to die, and will raise thee up unto myself,
Sura iii. 54-57. 'and will deliver thee from the unbelievers; 'and will make thy followers to be over those 'that disbelieve even until the day of judgment. Then 'unto me shall ye return; and I will judge between you, 'as to that concerning which ye have been at variance.

[1] I must note, however, that the passage quoted does not bear out his argument:—"O ye that believe, verily from amongst your wives and children, ye have enemies; wherefore beware of them": meaning, no doubt that they were dangerous because likely to tempt them from the right way; as Luke xiv. 26.

'But they that disbelieve, I will visit them with a grievous 'punishment, both in this world and the next; they shall 'have none to help them. But they that believe and 'do good works, we shall fulfil to them their reward. And 'God loveth not the transgressors. These signs (or verses) 'and this sage admonition do we rehearse unto thee.' Now may the Lord open thine eyes and understanding, for these are the very words of thy Master and his confession and testimony in the revelation which he claimed (and which thou admittest) to be from the Lord. Turn not then away from the right, for if thou wilt be true to thyself, the light shall spring upon thee."

Ministry of the Apostles, and spread of Christianity (161, 162).

Advancing now to the ministry of the Apostles,—after a brief notice of the descent of the Holy Ghost, "the Paraclete," on the day of Pentecost, and the gift of tongues, he proceeds:—"Upon that, the Apostles separated, each to the country to which he was called, and the language of which was made known unto him. And they wrote out the Holy Gospel, and the story and teaching of Christ, in every tongue at the dictation of the Holy Ghost. So the Nations drew near unto them, and believed their testimony; and, giving up the world and their false beliefs, embraced the Christian faith, as soon as ever the dawn of truth and light of the Good tidings broke upon them. Distinguishing thus the true from the false, and error from the right direction, they embraced the Gospel and held it fast without doubt or wavering, when they saw the wonderful works and signs of the Apostles, and their lives and conversation set after the holy and beautiful example of our Saviour, the traces whereof remain even unto the present day. From them, the Faith hath been handed down; we have added nothing to it, neither taken aught therefrom. In this Faith we shall live, in it we shall die, and in the same shall we rise again, and stand in the presence of Christ our Lord, in the day when the whole world shall be gathered before Him. How different this from the life of thy Master and his Companions, who ceased not to go forth in battle and rapine, to smite with the sword, to seize the little ones, and ravish wives and maidens,—plundering and laying waste, and carrying the people away into captivity! And this they continue unto the present day,—inciting men to these evil deeds, even as Omar the Caliph said,—*If one hath a heathen neighbour, and is in need of his price, let him seize and sell him.*[1] And many such things they say and teach. Look now at the lives of Simon and Paul, who went about healing the sick, and raising the dead, by the name of Christ our Lord; and mark the contrast."

Miracles no longer shown saving in individual and exceptional cases (162, 163).

If it be asked why the power of working miracles is no longer seen in our Holy men, our Apologist answers that their ministry differs from that of the Apostles who had to preach a new faith with extraordinary evidence. Miraculous cures, at the prayer of Holy men, are still performed in individual cases, to mark their acceptance with the Lord, and to show that the healing virtue is not dead. But if the practice were common of quickening the dead and healing the sick, then no one need die, and where then would be the promise of the Resurrection? Moreover, they are no longer required. Miracles were needed only in the first days of spreading the faith amongst nations sunk in idolatry and ignorance. Man is not to be forced by superfluous exhibitions of power, nor driven like the beasts by the appeal to his senses. Sufficient evidence had been long ago provided, and he was left, as a rational being in the exercise of his faculties to apply the same.

FINAL APPEAL (163-165).

"And now," concludes Al Kindy, "I have related to thee, very briefly, the story of our Saviour the Christ, with a short notice of his Apostles from whom we have received our blessed Faith and hold it fast. Now consider what thou wilt of that which I have set before thee, in connection with what thou already knowest of the same, and judge between us righteously. O if thou wouldest but listen to my advice, and, leaving what is

[1] I need hardly say that this sentiment is entirely at variance with the liberal and tolerant policy of Omar.

dark and evil, come to the light and brightness of the Gospel, then shouldest thou be of the number of our Saviour's chosen ones, inheriting the kingdom of heaven and that blessedness which knoweth no ending, and the joy of which passeth description. Fear Him, my Friend, who hath power both over the body and the soul, Who is ready to have mercy on thee, and embrace thee, even as a tender father embraceth his wandering son. The Lord hath favoured thee with wisdom and understanding above thy fellows. Be not then deceived with the pomps and vanities of this transitory life; for verily the world with its lusts and pleasures is a Syren that leadeth to destruction. Look to thy soul, my Friend, before the day when thy sight shall fail from thine eyes, and weigh well what I have written in the scales of justice and by the light of reason. The matter is one of infinite import, and cannot, without eternal risk, be put aside. It concerneth thee, not only in this life, but in the great future before thee, when no vain excuse will be accepted. And know of a certainty that he who rejecteth all vain and false securities, and believeth in the Lord, hath laid hold of a sure refuge, and will find eternal rest in His good pleasure.

Conclusion (164-165).

"I have now done my task to the best of my ability; and, having delivered my Message to the utmost of my power, I leave it with thee, and with all those who shall read this my Book,—praying the Lord to fulfil in thee, and in us all, every good work, redeem us from all iniquity, and join us hereafter in His kingdom above with the chosen ones whom he visiteth with His beneficence and grace.

"And now, Peace be on thee, and Mercy from the Lord, and His blessing! Amen."

STEPHEN AUSTIN AND SONS, PRINTERS, HERTFORD.

Art. XX.—*Further Note on the Apology of Al-Kindy.* By Sir W. Muir, K.C.S.I., D.C.L., LL.D.

With reference to my paper on the Apology of Al-Kindy, I have received the following letter from Professor Ignatius Guidi, dated Rome, 24th February:—

"You will be glad to hear that in the Propaganda Library (*Museo Borgiani*) I found a MS. of the Apology of Al-Kindî, together with the letter of his Moslem friend. The amanuensis was, I think, a Jacobite (the MS. is written in Karshuni character), hence he says (page 5, line 18 of the printed text): والنسطورية وهم اكفر القوم الخ .... واما اليقوبية اصحابك الخ [1] The Roman MS. is apparently of the same family with the Paris MS. as described by Zotenberg, *Catalogue des MSS. Syriaques de la Biblioth. Nationale,* Nos. 204, 205."

In a subsequent communication, dated 12th March, M. Ign. Guidi adds:—

"The Propaganda MS. of Al-Kindy's Apology has, at the end of the letter of the Moslem, a note which states that a certain Abuna Salîbâ ابونا الخوري صليبا abridged the letter of the Moslem; then a certain Mûsâ transcribed, from the copy of Abûnâ Salîbâ, the MS. now in the Propaganda, in the year of the Greeks 1957, corresponding with 1052 of the Hegira (1642–3 A.D.).

"The MS. is in octavo, and has 18 lines in every page; the letter of the Moslem occupies 16 pages; it seems therefore *to be a little* shorter than the printed text."

[1] That is to say, the Moslem advocate is made to represent the Nestorian as the worst, and the Jacobite the best, form of the Christian religion. The Arabic MSS. reverse this statement, and make Al-Kindy a Nestorian, which no doubt he was.

The notices referred to above from Zotenberg's Catalogue are as follows, pp. 155, 156:

"204. No. 8 (fol. 124*v.*) Apologie de la religion chrétienne, par un chrétien Jacobite (Jacque al Kindi) addressée, sous le forme de lettre, à un Musulman qui l'avait attaquée. En Carschouni; . . . .

"205. Apologie de la religione chrétienne, par Jacques le Kindien, Jacobite, en réponse à une attaque d'un Musulman de la famille de Haschim. En Carschouni . . . . Le préface est suivi de la lettre abrégée du Musulman. L'ouvrage proprement dit commence ainsi . . . . Cet exemplaire ne renferme pas la conclusion qui se trouve dans l'autre copie.

"Ce MS. a été exécuté en 1934 des Grecs (1619 de J.C.). La copie fut commencée par la diacre Salibi, de Damas, qui à abrégé lui-même la lettre Mahométane, et qui ajouté plusieurs notes marginales. La transcription a été continuée et terminée par son frere, le diacre Joané, et deux autres diacres, Serge et Moise.

". . . . . Il est à croire que l'ouvrage n'était pas designe par un titre particulier."

The Apology thus reaches us through the medium of MSS. belonging to two distinct families. *First*, the Arabic proper, handed down by the Nestorian section of the Church, which I take to be the original form in which the Apology appeared. *Secondly*, the Karshuny, or Arabic in Syriac character, handed down by the Jacobite Church;—which explains the appellation which I took to be a mistake in M. de Sacy's article (see p. vi of my paper).

The Karshuni family of MSS. is shown by Prof. Guidi's notes to have existed in a separate and independent form, at any rate Two and a half centuries ago.

www.ingramcontent.com/pod-product-compliance
Lightning Source LLC
Chambersburg PA
CBHW021417090426
42742CB00009B/1170

* 9 7 8 3 7 4 4 7 3 5 1 2 4 *